CIRCLES AND LINES

The William E. Massey Sr. Lectures in the History of American Civilization

2002

Circles and Lines

THE SHAPE OF LIFE
IN EARLY AMERICA

John Demos

HARVARD UNIVERSITY PRESS

Cambridge, Massachusetts, and London, England

2004

Library of Congress Cataloging-in-Publication Data

Demos, John.
Circles and lines : the shape of life in early America / John Demos.
p. cm — (the William E. Massey, Sr. lectures in
the history of American civilization ; 2002)
ISBN 0-674-01324-7 (hc : alk paper)
1. United States—Social life and customs—To 1775.
2. United States—Social life and customs—1783–1865.
I. Title.   II. Series.

E162.D46 2004
973—dc22
2003056917

To Io

(whose name holds the theme of this book)

with love and hope

Contents

Preface

ix

1. The Traditional World and the Logic of Circularity

1

2. The Transitional World and the Power of Novelty

25

3. The Modern World and the Rise of the Linear

57

Notes

87

Index

97

Preface

I would like to express my deep appreciation to Harvard University and its History of American Civilization Program for having asked me to deliver the 2002 William E. Massey Sr. Lectures. Truly, I felt honored by the invitation, and by the experience itself.

In some respects, my week on the Harvard campus seemed like a homecoming; I grew up just a few blocks away and am a grateful alumnus of the College and Graduate School. In that connection I want especially to acknowledge two remarkable teachers from my student days long ago: Oscar Handlin and Bernard Bailyn. Their example inspired me from the time I first thought of becoming a historian, and it inspires me still.

I should also like to acknowledge my parents, Raphael and Jean McMorran Demos, who were for several decades deeply engaged members of the Harvard community. I have thought about them often in direct relation to the theme of this book, since their lives could well be seen as extreme examples of the "linear" mode. For my father, the line began in a faraway ethnic enclave in Istanbul—"ethnic" because he

grew up Greek in that extraordinary Turkish metropolis—
and then went basically west for several thousand miles. For
my mother, it began on a remote piece of homesteaded
property overlooking the Pend d'Oreille River in the northern part of the state of Washington and eventually went east
for an almost equivalent distance, until their two lines inter-
sected at Harvard. Of course, without that intersection neither my Massey Lectures nor the present book could have
happened.

My most immediate acknowledgment is to a host of
friends, fellow scholars, and fellow writers. The central idea
in what follows is not an invention, or discovery, of my
own; indeed, it appears (to one degree or another) in the
work of a good many different people. My aim is to situate
it in a somewhat different way. For I do think it has belonged mostly to intellectual historians, those whose province is the study of high-level thought. In contrast, my own
approach is that of a social historian, concerned chiefly with
the ground-level experience of Ordinary Folk. Thus the basic shift I seek to effect: from high-level to ground-level,
from thought to behavior and experience. Of course, this
distinction is not absolute; the levels are interconnected at
many points. Moreover, thought is itself a form of behavior;
and most behavior involves thought at some point along
the way.

Half a dozen historian-friends provided detailed, and
highly beneficial, readings of the original Lectures manu-
script: Joyce Appleby, Doron Ben-Atar, Richard Brown, Jon
Butler, Rhys Isaac, Robert Johnston. I have received similar
benefit from my anthropologist-friend Robert LeVine, my
psychologist-wife Virginia Demos, and my writer-son-in-

law Michael Eilperin. Others, including at least three current dissertation students, have shared important work of their own that intersects directly with my "circles and lines" theme. Still others responded to email queries on a variety of specific points. (I'm especially grateful for suggestions received in that way from Robert St. George.) And many more contributed to my thinking in the remarkably lively discussions that followed each lecture. I regret that I cannot specifically name them all. My acknowledgment, in any case, *is* to all.

J.D.
Tyringham, Massachusetts
NOVEMBER 2003

CIRCLES AND LINES

I

The Traditional World and
the Logic of Circularity

The eye is the first circle; the horizon which it forms is the second; and throughout Nature this primary figure is repeated without end. It is the highest emblem in the cipher of the world. St. Augustine described the nature of God as a Circle whose center was everywhere and its circumference nowhere. We are all our lifetime reading the copious sense of this first of forms.[1]

In 1840 the philosopher Ralph Waldo Emerson opened an essay entitled "Circles" with these lines. Emerson's "first of forms" can serve also as a starting point here. But it does seem necessary to change the perspective somewhat: to move from philosophy to everyday experience, from intellectual to social history, and, as part of the same maneuver, from the nineteenth back to the seventeenth and eighteenth centuries.

Consider, then, certain very basic elements in the experience of virtually everyone in the historical venue that we commonly refer to as colonial America. These are all, in one way or another, circles—versions of Emerson's "primary figure, repeated without end." And "basic" is the fully operative term for them—indeed, so basic, so much a taken-for-granted part of Life, that almost no one felt a need to comment on them. Which means that we, a few hundred years later on, have to pry them out of the very bedrock of existence in that seemingly remote and alien time.

But the evidence we need is not, after all, so hard to find. Here is a kind of fragment—very small and specific, even homely, one of many such we could conceivably extract from the bedrock, all with approximately the same underlying theme. In the year 1670, the General Court of the Massachusetts Bay Colony enacted a policy meant to control a mounting problem of inflation in wages and prices.[2] In taking this action, the Court made certain distinctions between the wages appropriate for ordinary day-laborers at different times of the year. They ordered, for instance, that the maximum wage allowable in June (midsummer) would be 2 shillings per day, whereas in December (midwinter) it would be 1 shilling, 3 pence. Why did they arrange things this way? Pretty clearly, it had to do with the length of the workday (June versus December). Converting the numbers into the same coin—which, in this case, would be pennies—yields a ratio between the two wage levels of 24 to 15. And, as it happens, 24 to 15 is also exactly the ratio of the hours of daylight—*sun*light—at these two opposite points on the calendar, in the latitude that Massachusetts occupies.

Consider another fragment of evidence. When one looks in local records from early America—for example, in court records, where notations of time are especially likely to appear—one often finds such notations made by reference to the sun. A typical example might begin: "as I was coming out of the south field about twilight . . . "; "when my wife was suckling her child a little after daybreak . . . "; "about mid-day, when the sun was high . . . " By putting these fragments together (and there are many more), we can begin to feel the importance in these people's lives not just of the sun as such but of the sun's *movement,* its regular comings and goings across the sky. In fact, it seems entirely clear that dawn and dusk, sunup and sundown, were the two most important markers in the overall scheme of their day.

We can go on to imagine the meaning of those markers for specific forms of activity and experience. There was work (as already suggested by that bit of Massachusetts wage-and-price legislation). There were mealtimes. (These, too, were linked to the hours of daylight; for the most part, you wouldn't eat after dark, and that meant some changes in meal scheduling dependent on the seasons.) And, at the broadest, most basic level of all, there was the whole cycle of sleep and wakefulness—which, for certain, was much more tightly linked to night and day than is the case for most of us in century twenty-one.[3] (Of course, our lives also conform, in general terms, to the same sequencing. But we can, and we do, move specific activities around rather freely in relation to night and day. One sees especially striking examples of this on college campuses: "all-nighters" and such.)

Moreover, the point here—the contrast between our way and theirs—is actually deeper still. In a sense, we can make daytime and nighttime experience continuous: the one passes into the other, and we hardly have to notice. But for the people of colonial America, as for premodern people everywhere, this was a hugely significant transition. For them, the main thing about daytime and nighttime was *dis*continuity—and not just discontinuity in what they could or couldn't do, but also in the very boundaries of experience. When night fell, the boundaries contracted enormously, so as to enclose, in the typical case, just a single household at a time. The neighbors—all the folk with whom, in the daytime, one had worked or bartered or gossiped—were now, and throughout the period of darkness to come, set apart. In a sense, experience at night was privatized: each man, woman, or child enclosed within his or her own family. Then, next morning when the sun came up, the boundaries expanded again, and one's ties to the wider community were restored. That recurrent change was itself an important rhythm of premodern life.

But even this does not quite get to the bottom of it. For the differences embraced not just the practical side of things, but also attitudes, and emotions, and one's fundamental sense of the world. Here is another fragment—or, actually, a little cluster of fragments—taken from the records of early American witchcraft cases. The dangers and injuries most often attributed to witchcraft fell into two distinct categories. One of these could be headlined "accidents": surprising and upsetting events, such as a snake abruptly appearing in the roadway and biting your horse's leg as you rode along; or cutting yourself with a scythe while mowing your field (something you had done a thousand times before without difficulty); or finding that your beer had suddenly gone rancid in the basement barrel. In fact, the list of such possibilities was extremely long and variable, with the common element of inconvenient, or painful, mischance.

A second category included what might be called "mysteries": for instance, spectral shapes darting about a room; weird and terrifying sounds; and other such famously witchy happenings. A small group of examples, taken directly from court testimony, will serve to convey the flavor.[4]

Thursday night, being about the 27th day of November, we heard a great noise without against the house, whereupon myself and [my] wife looked out, and [we] saw nobody. Yet soon after, the like noise was heard upon the roof of the house . . . [It went on and on for several hours; they called it poltergeist.]

Goody Harrison [the name of an accused witch] appeared in my bedchamber . . . in the night, just before my child was stricken ill; and I said "the Lord bless me, here is Goody Harrison." And the child lying on the outside, I took it and laid it between me and my husband; and the child continued strangely ill for about three weeks, and then died. [This one is a kind of ghost story, with apparently fatal consequence.]

Presently, when all were asleep, I was pressed by a great weight on my chest as I lay on my bed, and I tried to cry out but could not, for I was choked strangely. [We might see this as a paralyzing panic attack; they saw it as witchcraft.]

One could find many more examples, but the underlying point is already clear. The "accidents" were usually things that happened in the daytime; they were indeed upsetting, even injurious, but they also had a straightforward, practical aspect. The "mysteries"—the shapes, the spectres, and so on—were much scarier and almost always happened at night. The difference points toward a deeper opposition, in the minds of these people, between darkness and light (night and day). In fact, a great deal of traditional folklore, originating long before the American colonial period, featured the same associations. Goblins, ghosts, and werewolves—not to mention witches themselves—were notoriously creatures of the night. The Devil was typically described as "the Prince of Darkness." (One finds that term again and again in the witchcraft records, in sermons, in private writings as well.) Darkness itself was a kind of all-purpose metaphor for evil; there is a line in Shakespeare's *Julius Caesar* to the effect that nighttime is "when evils are most free." Even sleep could be strangely frightening; at least dreams could be frightening, given their special aura of contact with the supernatural.

Here is yet another deeply resonant comment from the period: an English minister writes that in dreams "the table of our heart is turned into an index of iniquities, and all our thoughts are nothing but texts to condemn us." With a little adjustment to remove the judgmental tone, one might even see that statement as anticipating Freud's idea of the relation between dreaming and the repressed unconscious. In sum, nighttime stood for a whole darker side of life (that metaphor again)—for the fear and mystery of the unknown, for danger, and, at some level, for death itself (death being the ultimate darkness). And daytime, in contrast, meant safety, a sense of assurance, the enjoyment of things familiar and comfortable.

It seems necessary, before leaving this matter of the daily (or "diurnal") cycle, to say a bit more about belief, and practice, in the measurement of time.[5] But in order to get this right, one has to take a very long view of history, starting with classical Greece and Rome. Sundials are the oldest form of time measurement; they may actually have predated Greece and Rome. Next come water clocks and sand glasses, both operating on the principle of a substance—water or sand—flowing at a supposedly regular pace from one receptacle to another. (To be sure, in practice such regularity was often very hard to achieve.) Each of these systems was designed to reflect rhythms intrinsic to Nature—the sundial most obviously and directly, the others by way of linkage to time as measured on the sundial. But perhaps the most crucial element here, lasting until well into the Middle Ages, was the use of (so-called) "flexible hours"—the custom of dividing the daytime into twelve equal units, based on its overall length. This meant shorter hours in winter, longer hours in summer, and *different* hours for every single day of the year. Then, in the thirteenth century, came the invention of mechanical clocks—and, in the centuries to follow, their gradual refinement and improvement—so as to produce a wholly different experience of time. One of the key results was that "flexible hours" became inflexible (of the same length) and thus no longer directly connected to the sun and daylight.

Lewis Mumford, among others, has given the invention of the clock a place of importance for the history of Western culture right alongside the printing press. Here is how he put it in his deservedly famous work *Technics and Civilization:* "When one thinks of the day as an abstract span of time, one does not go to bed with the chickens on a winter's night; one invents wicks, chimneys, lamps, gaslights, electric lamps, so as to use all the hours belonging to the day. When one thinks of time not as a sequence of experiences, but as a collection of hours, minutes, and seconds, the habits of adding time and saving time come into existence."[6]

But this last is the end of a several-centuries-long process of historical change. So the question becomes: where did colonial Americans fit into the process? Throughout the seventeenth century the sundial was probably their only nonintuitive means of time-telling. (There were a few exceptions; the Boston market, for example, boasted a public clock as early as 1660.) In the eighteenth century, tower clocks did begin to appear here and there—on churches, in urban centers—and pocket watches, too, among the wealthy. But for the vast majority of plain folk in early America, suntime was the only available standard. When ministers and other authorities spoke about time, they typically said that it "belonged to God," or that it expressed "Nature's regulating power." Of course, God and Nature amounted, in their minds, to virtually the same thing; and neither one followed the clock.

There were other cycles that also served to organize their lives. One that seems very alien and obscure to us today is the lunar cycle, the regular waxing and waning of the moon over the span of a little more than 28 days. Its importance is reflected in a leading period print genre, the almanac. Almanacs were everywhere in colonial America, starting from far back in the seventeenth century. And almanacs were full of moon-based information. A typical example refers on the frontispiece to "The Rising, Setting, and Southing of the moon." And, on its inside pages, each month's "table" begins with an account of the moon's phases: new moon, first quarter, full moon, last quarter.[7]

Perhaps the lunar cycle was related—in the actual experience of women, and at least symbolically for men—to the biological rhythm of the menses (the time frame being roughly the same). Indeed, this apparent link has been acknowledged since ancient times, etymologically and otherwise. The menses, moreover, may well have evoked a deeper, more encompassing element in women's lives: the regular cycle of conception, pregnancy, birthing, and (back to) preconceptive status. As this sequence recurred perhaps eight to a dozen times in the average case, its own "circular" power must have seemed huge.

The lunar cycle may also have had more immediate and practical implications. Consider the origins of our term "moonlighting" as a way of referring to a second line of work. On clear nights, when the moon was completely or nearly full, a blacksmith or a wheelwright might chop wood and perform other outdoor chores for a neighboring farmer. At other points in the lunar month, of course, this was impossible.

Consider, too, another period artifact, similar in structure to almanacs yet quite different in content. Traditionally known as "the Book of Knowledge," it was, in any case, all about the moon. Here is a brief sample of what appeared in one such: "On the 15th day of the moon, you must begin no work; it is a grievous day. A sick man shall long travail, but he shall escape. A child born [on this day] shall die young. That which is lost shall be found. To let blood is good."[8] Similar comments attached to all the other "days of the moon." In effect, then, this was a premodern "how-to" guide, a compendium of predictions and pointers useful in everyday decision-making. It anticipated—and, at the same time, prescribed for—many sorts of common experience (illness, the ancient remedy of bloodletting, a child's future, losing and finding valuable objects), each one linked to particular parts of the lunar cycle. How often people put such nostrums into practice—how often, in short, they actually made choices based on the moon—we cannot say. The strongest evidence of that link involves farming—the days chosen to plant, for example.[9] And the mindset itself is indicative.

We turn next to another fundamental rhythm in their lives, for which the evidence is overwhelming: the annual cycle, the movement of the seasons. This had numerous different dimensions, some obvious, others relatively obscure (but not, for that reason, unimportant). Perhaps the most obvious was the matter of physical—that is, bodily—sensation, especially as regards temperature change. In summer they were warm, in winter they were cold, far beyond anything we typically experience. They could be cold, for instance, right inside their houses and public buildings; Cotton Mather, the famous Boston minister, wrote in his diary of having to skim ice off the water in the baptismal font in his church on winter mornings.

Another obvious, and hugely extensive, aspect of the seasonal cycle was work itself—especially the varieties of agricultural work in which the vast majority of colonial Americans were regularly engaged. Of course, the details of all this varied considerably from one region to another. In New England the cycle was especially complex, as farmers sought to combine the cultivation of grains, vegetables, and fruit with the raising and care of domestic animals. Further south, seasonal calendars were tightly geared to staple-crop production: tobacco in the Chesapeake, rice and indigo in the Carolinas. Each setting had its own particular configuration of tasks and responsibilities. And each showed important season-to-season differences, not just of substance but also of pacing.[10] Virtually everywhere, harvest was a peak time—a crisis even—when all hands, including those of women and children, were turned to getting the crops safely in. But there were slack times, too, especially in winter, when things slowed way down for days or weeks at a stretch.

The same agricultural rhythm meant changes also in food availability. People experienced dramatic seasonal differences in everyday diet—moving, say, from the summertime, with lots of fresh vegetables and fruit, to the special bounty of harvest, traditionally celebrated with a feast of freshly slaughtered animals (the antecedent of our own Thanksgiving), and then to winter, when the dietary range would narrow to dried foods like peas and turnips and a dwindling supply of salted meats.[11]

A different (though not unrelated) kind of seasonal variance involved health and illness and marriage and reproduction. The evidence for this lies mostly below the surface and must be pried out through laborious demographic analysis, but its impact was certainly large. For example, marriage-making—weddings—showed a striking seasonal distribution. The headline is that weddings happened in hugely disproportionate numbers during the late fall.[12] And, going a bit further, one finds a distinct up-and-down annual "curve" for weddings (see Figure 1), with much regularity from one year and one community to the next. Moreover, the distance between top and bottom was very wide; there were roughly three times as many weddings in November, for example, as during the midsummer low. This particular curve was not so directly tied to Nature's rhythms as, for instance, all the activity around farming. It could even be seen as culturally determined—since people might well have chosen differently about when to marry. Still, the link to harvest seems too obvious to ignore. When that was over, there was suddenly more time available, and more energy; there was also a feeling of release, and expansiveness, and good cheer. The impulse to celebrate might then lead not just to a Thanksgiving feast but to a wedding as well.

And there was more. This next had no aspect of cultural preference but was entirely controlled by Nature—in fact, by deep (and not fully understood) elements of human biology. It's what demographers call the "conception cycle"; and it reflects the way pregnancies were unevenly, but very consistently, distributed throughout the calendar year. The evidence of copious local and family records yields another annual curve—in fact, a pair of curves, one reflecting births, the second, times of conception (see Figure 2). Of course,

Jan Feb Mar Apr May Jun Jul Aug Sep Oct Nov Dec

1. Wedding cycle.

the dynamic element here was always conception; once that had taken place, birth would (barring mishap) occur about nine months later. In fact, the curve shows two peaks in conception, the tallest coming in late spring, with corresponding valleys (and a difference between them approaching 100 percent).[13]

What this meant, in terms of actual experience, was many more babies born in late winter than at other times of the year. In fact, demographers have found the same rhythm in premodern communities throughout the northern hemisphere. Moreover, they have also found it in the southern hemisphere—except that there the months, though not the seasons, are directly reversed. The southern conception peak comes in November-December, which, of course, is their spring; so the pattern is actually the same. We might just note, as a final gloss on all this, that the conception cycle flattens out and virtually disappears in the modern period. The reason is obvious: as soon as *contra*ception enters the picture—that is, planned fertility control—the timing of pregnancy is determined by innumerable individual choices; and those choices, when aggregated, spread evenly throughout the year.

2. Birth and conception cycle.

Death and illness showed another, equally distinctive, seasonal profile (see Figure 3). A late-spring peak, mainly affecting adults, was linked primarily to pulmonary illness—for example, pneumonia and tuberculosis—which in turn reflected reduced nutritional levels during the late winter and early spring. A second peak, in late summer, centered on intestinal disorders that particularly affected children. Stagnant water, spoiled food, and atmospheric conditions of high heat and humidity offered a favorable environment for the pathogens behind various forms of dysentery and diarrhea (in period terminology, "the flux"). A related factor, also in the late summer and especially important to the south, was mosquito-borne diseases such as malaria ("fevers and agues") or yellow fever. By contrast, midwinter, which must have been difficult in so many other ways, was actually the least dangerous season from the standpoint of illness.[14]

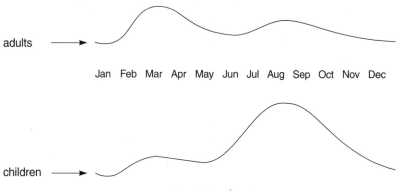

adults

Jan Feb Mar Apr May Jun Jul Aug Sep Oct Nov Dec

children

3. Death and illness cycle.

We can now bring together all these different elements of seasonal variance in a final summary review. Depending on the calendar, you *felt* differently (especially in terms of cold and warmth); you *ate* different foods (and in some periods you could be quite hungry, while in others you were abundantly supplied); you *worked* very different schedules, at different tasks. And in addition, you couldn't help but notice, within your local surroundings, many sick and dying children at some points in the year, and sick and dying adults at other points; a lot more babies born in certain months than in others; a regular post-harvest spike in weddings; and so on. Almost certainly, too, there were other seasonal cycles that historians haven't yet recovered—perhaps in matters like socializing and courtship; possibly in the frequency (and severity) of personal violence (including legally punishable crime); very likely in patterns of travel and trade over long distances, especially in the northernmost latitudes, where winters would be long and harsh. (To take just one small example: a rural Massachusetts clergyman complained that he could never get news of the outside world in wintertime; it was too snowy, and the roads became impassable.)[15] In short, we don't *know* all the dimensions of seasonal patterning in early America, but without any doubt they shaped experience across a very broad range. People would routinely, and instinctively, orient themselves to everyday life by where they were on the calendar.

There is one more cycle to be joined to this assemblage: the *life* cycle, the way these early American folk conceptualized, and organized, the sequence of all their personal experience, from its beginning clear through to its end. Right away we can notice metaphorical connectives to certain of the other rhythms already considered. Thus, early Americans often spoke of life's "morning" and "evening" (the diurnal cycle), or its "waxing" and "waning" phases (the lunar cycle). And most of all, perhaps, they used the figure of "the seasons of life"; a full lifetime was like the complete rotation of a calendar year, with its intrinsic parts of spring, summer, fall, and winter.

The life cycle could also be rendered visually—as, for example, in an English print dated to 1733 (see Figure 4). We have nothing similar from eighteenth-century America; still, this image certainly reflected prevalent attitudes on both sides of the Atlantic in that time period. Notice especially its nonlinear shape; it resembles a double-sided staircase, with an up-slope for the first half of life and a downslope for the second. Moreover, if one includes the lower section of the drawing—with a christening scene underneath the staircase just to the left of center, and a burial scene also underneath but just to the right—it rounds off and almost forms a circle. It thus positions the starting-point and the end-point, birth and death, as adjacent to one another: "ashes to ashes, and dust to dust," in the familiar Biblical phrase.

Furthermore, the image makes no attempt to depict well-defined "phases" or "stages"; instead, it presents a rather mechanical schedule of ten-year intervals. This suggests a fuzzy, unarticulated view of the parts of the life cycle—as if one shaded into the next, and numbers (of years) were the most plausible way to mark the changes. In truth, eighteenth-century folk did have some life-cycle terminology; and they

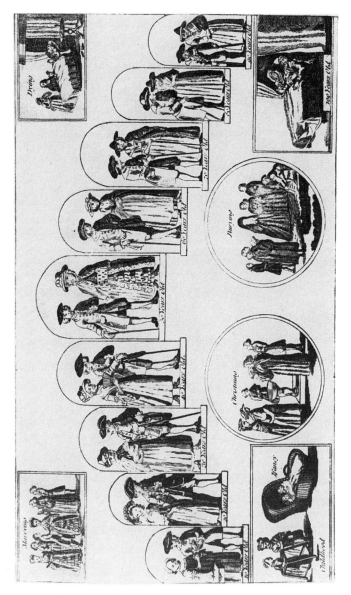

4. Life cycle (English print, "The Ages of Man," dated 1733).

used it, up to a point. In particular, they used "infancy" and "childhood" (both of which appear at the extreme lower left of the drawing); they also used "old age" for the downside of the staircase. Moreover, they had one additional phase-related term, "youth" (as they typically said). This, however, was especially loose and vague; youth could extend to age 30 or even beyond. There was vagueness, too, in its experiential meaning; a youth was anyone on the way to adulthood and preparing for adulthood—with none of the special coloration that we nowadays find in our own term "adolescence." Meanwhile, a term they did *not* much have was "middle age." Maybe they would have recognized it, but they almost never used it.[16]

Here is another image—but in words, not a picture—from a long piece of verse writing by the early New England poet Anne Bradstreet. Its title is "The Four Ages of Man"—so Bradstreet does set out to specify the parts of the life cycle more or less as distinct phases (or, in her phrasing, "ages"). The poem begins as follows:

> Lo, now, four others act upon the stage,
> Childhood, and youth; the manly, and old age.[17]

What Bradstreet does here is most revealing. She uses ostensibly developmental (or phase-related) terms for the first, second, and fourth of her "ages," but something else for the third. She calls it "the manly." That's not a reference to gender; what she means is "manlike"—or, better still, "humanlike." In Bradstreet's way of thinking (and she can stand also for many others), the third part of the life cycle, the entirety of what we would call the middle years, was not actually a phase at all. Rather, it was the apex, the epitome of (so to speak) "humanhood"—a time when one was simply a *fully developed person.* As such, it was a standard against which childhood and youth, on one side, and old age, on the other, would appear as deviations. Perhaps those other times were "phases" in life's movement—either on the way up or on the way back down. But the middle years were simply the top. In fact, this life-cycle imagery corresponded with many sorts of actual experience. If one were to plot the distribution of wealth in relation to age, or public office-holding in relation to age, the result would look much like the staircase drawing: men of fifty or so on top, with younger and older men sloping away (and down) on either side.

To be sure, these last points are specifically about *men.* And there is considerable evidence of difference for women of comparable age—evidence that suggests both inward and outward distress. The records of court cases, for example, yield a skewed picture of participation by women in the middle years: they were disproportionately present as defendants (and convicts), and nearly absent as witnesses (in actions around other principals). Members of the same cohort were especially prominent in witchcraft proceedings; often they were targets—and yet also were prime sources—of the most damaging forms of accusation. Moreover, the qualitative details in witchcraft testimony reveal a special center of preoccupation: with maternal function, with personal (especially bodily) integrity, with "theft" and the loss of essential powers. This overall configuration draws attention to the experience—and cultural meaning—of menopause. Recall that early American women bore children for as long as they were biologically able; thus, menopause was vividly marked in each of their lives. Note, too, that such women were largely defined by their reproductive powers—following the Biblical injunction to "be fruitful, and multiply, and replenish the earth." A menopausal woman was, by this measure, one who had lost her "fruitfulness" and who might never thereafter find as significant a social role.[18]

In sum, the situation of midlife women was ambiguous, even contradictory. On the one hand, they shared quite substantially in the power and influence of their male peers, as "helpmeets," and "mistresses," and managers of large households. But on the other, they seem also to have experienced a distinct downside, centered on the end of childbearing. In effect, then, the life-cycle image of the staircase, so apt in the case of men, worked less well with women. For them, the platform on top had a kind of trapdoor.

Let me pause here to invoke—and maybe to apologize for—a rather ponderous phrase that appears up front in the title of this section. "The Logic of Circularity" seems quite a mouthful, but all it really means is the way many things fitted together: "logic," then, in the sense of a system; logic, as a matter of coherence and connection; logic, too, as a way of moving our focus somewhat more toward attitudes, values, and ideas. This was advertised as a ground-level tour; but now we can elevate at least a bit—from the feet, one might say, to the heart, and head, and brain.

Actually, the life cycle forms a kind of bridge between these two levels—since the life cycle is a concept as well as a set of experiences. And next we might inquire: what did people think and do when the regularity of one or another of the various cycles was broken by some unusual event? Invariably this would happen from time to time: an eclipse would darken the sun for a portion of a particular day; or there would be an entire season without any rain; or clouds of locusts would suddenly arrive one midsummer morning and eat up the crops as they ripened in the field; or an outbreak of epidemic illness would strike in wintertime, when ordinarily people did not so often get sick. Or, on the positive side, an entire year might pass without any of the regular sickly periods. These events, whatever their specific nature, took on significance from the very fact that they were unusual—they stood out because they ran counter to the familiar cyclical rhythms. Hence they called for special pondering and, ultimately, for interpretation—as "signs" and symbols of supernatural purpose (or, in period terminology, as "providences").

The formula went this way: Nature is basically regular, predictable, cyclical; and when it *isn't* like that, forces outside Nature—*super*Nature—must be actively in play. Therefore: after eclipses, dry spells, locust infestations, and epidemics, and also after uncommonly healthy seasons, these people would respond by declaring what, in effect, were special days-off: "days of fasting" (for the difficult times) and "days of thanksgiving" (for the happier ones), during which they explicitly acknowledged the *extra*ordinary nature of what had happened. It was as if the Almighty had communicated with them through the events, and now they wished to communicate back. Again, the interesting point for our purposes is the way these exchanges depended on the cycles of everyday experience. Without a clear understanding of what was usual and natural, one couldn't properly recognize those things that were *un*usual—and therefore *super*natural.

The "logic of circularity" hooked up with much else in

their lives as well. Their ideas about governance, for example, expressed at bottom an all-encompassing principle of conservatism. Government was expected to conserve the traditional wisdom of society, to reinstate—and, indeed, to recycle—old laws and old policies. It would not be a creative force or even a means of formulating new strategies to meet changing circumstances. (That, more or less, is our own idea.) Instead, for them government served as the guardian of values and procedures that were literally "tried and true."

Something similar was characteristic of the productive economy, especially in its local manifestations. Prevailing views made economic activity into a zero-sum game. What went around and around—and most of their production, and their consumption too, was, of course, tightly linked to the annual cycle—could only add up to the same total in the long run. By contrast, our own striving for economic growth and development would have seemed dangerous, or downright immoral, to them. And morality was keyed to many parts of their productive system, as a virtual guarantor of steady-state goals.

History—their ideas about, and attitudes toward, history—can be fitted to the same model. Invariably, they stressed the educative function of history, its value as a storehouse of lessons and examples. In this way of thinking, the past generally prefigured and predicted both present and future. Therefore a wise man—one who wished to remain comfortably attuned to his surroundings—would always pay careful attention to history and its teachings. Moreover, those who pondered history in a more systematic way saw cyclical movement as its underlying principle. Lord Bolingbroke, the eighteenth-century theorist who was read and appreciated throughout the English-speaking world, wrote as follows: "The best instituted governments . . . carry in them the seeds of their own destruction; and though they grow and improve for a time, they will soon tend visibly to their dissolution. Every hour they live is an hour the less that they have to live." And a colonial governor, writing near the end of the century, made the same claim by directly invoking the metaphor of the life cycle. "Experience proves that political bodies, like the animal economy, have their periods of infancy, youth, maturity, decay, and dissolution."[19]

We haven't much dealt with the subject of religion here. Yet, of course, religious beliefs and values informed this people's understanding of politics, economics, history—and just about everything else. In truth, early American religious history seems, for the present subject, to cut both ways. Certainly, one could argue that Protestant Christianity—in its numerous American versions—showed a strong linear component. This would be especially true for groups like the Puritans that lived with the fervent expectation of "millennial" outcomes. In their view, human history was (as Jonathan Edwards put it) a "work of redemption," a work to be completed, sooner or later, by the Second Coming of Christ and the establishment of God's everlasting kingdom. Thus a line, or perhaps an arrow, pointed from a highly deficient *here* toward a transcendently glorious *there.*

Still, the big tent of Protestant religion offered room for more cyclical elements as well. The Bible itself, especially the Old Testament, is full of cyclical teaching: "The sun ariseth, and the sun goeth down . . . The wind goeth to the south, and turneth about unto the north . . . The thing that hath been, it is that which shall be." Indeed, it was quite possible to incorporate even millennial goals into a fundamentally circular viewpoint. From Adam and Eve in the Garden, into and past the Fall, descending, then, through countless generations of disappointment and failure and sin, and finally back *up* to the Second Coming and its glorious accompaniments—redemption as *restoration:* for many Protestant folk of Early America, that was indeed the fundamental shape of the cosmos.

This is almost the end-point of our "circles" discussion. But before we finally get there, we need to register a kind of caution. To be honest, what's been offered so far is something of an overstatement. It actively embraces those elements of early American life and culture that conformed most closely to cyclical principles. And it largely avoids other elements that might seem to have expressed a different principle. The title of this first part is "The Traditional World," and, of the next, "The Transitional World." But in fact the "traditional" should probably be seen as a kind of abstraction that exaggerates and oversimplifies the complex realities of early American life. When one looks at such realities in detail, the "transitional" appears to have been already under way. (Certainly, it was under way in the eighteenth century.) And, in the next part, that's where we must start back in—not exactly by withdrawing the points already made, but rather by shading them here and there, with the further aim, too, of putting this whole lumbering *gestalt* of early American history into some sort of forward motion across time.

2

The Transitional World and the Power of Novelty

In picking up the threads of this necessarily sprawling discussion, we need to make a pair of strategic adjustments. The first is a narrowing of focus. In the previous chapter we tried to cover a huge expanse of historical turf, centered on colonial America but also extending way out to include a lot of (what might be called) traditional culture in the premodern world. From now on, we'll be pointing more and more toward things distinctively American. The second is also a narrowing move, but of a different sort. Where there are so many threads, it may be helpful to take particular hold of one and see, in some detail, where it leads.

What comes next, then, is a single-thread unraveling of the history of novelty—especially, of attitudes toward novelty—from the Age of Discovery up through the early nineteenth century. And it starts with a bit of personal memory. Picture a dusty schoolyard, surrounded by as yet unfinished classrooms, on the outskirts of a little village in West Africa. A young American, cast in the role of Peace Corps volunteer, has just completed his first day of work and is walking toward another unfinished building—the faculty apartment complex—when a student approaches. "Please, sir," the student begins, "America is my favorite country; can you help me go there?" Taken a little aback by this direct (but entirely friendly) appeal, the teacher asks why America should be a favorite country. To which the student responds, with an air of absolute assurance: "Because, sir, everything is so *new* there."

This scene is almost as vivid to me today as it was when it happened forty years ago. I remember how confused and jarred I felt by my student's comment; indeed, the irony of comment and context could hardly have been stronger. There I was, standing amid those half-formed structures, on a site that had been bush country just months before, in a school which had opened its doors for the first time earlier that day, among students who were in some cases innocent of any prior learning. I had arrived the previous week (on a road that was itself freshly built), more or less in the vanguard of a vast program of educational expansion, all in the name of the New Africa. I thought I had never before seen so much that was new; yet my student spoke admiringly of the newness of America.

Newness is actually a very old story in America; we can take it right back to Columbus. Our textbooks say that when Columbus "discovered" America, he didn't know what it was. He was anticipating a landfall in the Orient, and he hopefully called the native people he encountered "Indians." In fact, he may have known more than he first let on; but this conventional account, whether or not it falsifies Columbus, serves to identify a deeper truth about the process of discovery. Europeans of that bygone era—far more medieval than modern in spirit—did not expect to discover new lands, new peoples, new principles, new forms of community. This was, of course, the essence of their traditional outlook—the world as a known, and basically a fixed, entity. Theirs was a worldview based on long-established boundaries, generally stable contents, and structural principles inherited from time-out-of-mind.

One sign of all this was their difficulty in describing the New World, even after they realized that it wasn't part of the old one. Again and again, the explorers of America struggled to make word-pictures of their experience—initially for their colleagues and patrons at home, then, increasingly, for the wider literate public. Yet these pictures, when examined today, seem vague, fuzzy, platitudinous—not to say unreal. In part, the problem was one of description in the narrow sense, reflecting a lack of literary and linguistic conventions sufficient to deal with such unfamiliar material. But there was also a problem of perception, in a broader sense. Briefly put: they had a hard time seeing the New World straight, for what it truly was.[1]

In fact, to read the literature of exploration is to enter a kind of dream world, in which size, shape, color—indeed, every aspect of sense perception—seems distorted. Moreover, like most dream worlds, this one runs to positive and negative extremes; in effect, it's polarized. On the one hand, the New World appears a paradise, a "garden" full of natural bounty and beauty, where life is happier, sweeter, longer than anything known elsewhere. On the other hand, it's a special sort of Hell, a "wilderness" that teems with fearsome beasts, savage men (cannibals, for instance), and all manner of lurking danger. These two pictures—"image" and "anti-image," as Howard Mumford Jones called them many years ago—compete directly with one another in at least a century's worth of exploration literature. And there is little enough in between—little, that is, of intermediate positions where opportunity and danger, good and evil, are combined in a real-world blend. But to repeat: the New World was *not* the real world for most sixteenth-century Europeans. Instead, it was more like a giant fantasy screen on which their highest hopes and darkest fears stood sharply projected. Historians who study this material are not unlike clinicians amassing Rorschach protocols. Which is almost to say that in its origins America was a kind of ink blot, before it became an actual place!

We must now make a rapid switch from the period of "discovery" to the period of "settlement," and thus from problems of perception and description to problems of survival and adaptation. At the same time, we can twist the focus another notch or two, so as to move from the New World as a whole toward those regions within it that eventually became the United States.

Virtually all the earliest European settlements in North America—from Spanish Florida, through English Virginia and Dutch New Netherland, right up to Puritan New England—began under circumstances of extreme difficulty. There were "starving times" (as they themselves put it). There were grave political and social disorders. There was death and misery all around. In most cases, the worst of these experiences passed within a few years; but even then, and for decades thereafter, life in the new communities was laborious, unpredictable, sometimes cruel. The settlers responded to such conditions with a curious mix of courage and terror. The courage—in some cases, "nonchalance" might be a better word—was manifest in the way they attacked their difficulties: attacked the wilderness and cleared it, so as to build their dwellings and plant their crops; attacked the native peoples (Indians) whenever they felt crossed or threatened; attacked the problem of social disarray by creating ad hoc systems of authority and control.

If we stand back and think about it, the sheer strength—the *chutzpah*—in their response seems extraordinary. These were people, after all, with no prior experience of a woodland environment; people who had never known others of different race, language, and culture; people who were apparently unprepared for any aspect of community building. Trying to imagine myself as one of them, I think I would have been shaking in my shoes. Occasionally, to be sure, fear and a sense of desperation do break through in their own accounts of their experience. "Oh, that you did see my daily and hourly sighs, groans, and tears," wrote a young man in Virginia to his parents back in England. "I thought no head had been able to hold so much water . . . as doth flow from mine eyes."[2] But this man's reaction seems not to have been the predominant one. Indeed, it's my strong impression that most of the settlers managed somehow to shut out the danger, the isolation, the strangeness of it all. There was an element of "denial" in the way they carried on. Or—to make the same point in somewhat different terms—they were remarkably impervious to "otherness" of many kinds. Perhaps if they'd had our sensitivity in that respect, they might not have survived at all.

To speak of otherness is to circle back on the issue of novelty. One needs to realize that none of these early settlements were conceived as new departures in social experience—if by "new" is meant "other," in the sense of being different from received traditions and precedents. The Virginia colony, for example, was at the outset a business project, an extension of English mercantile enterprise, with a community and governmental structure that mirrored sixteenth-century "plantations" in Ireland. The founders of New England might seem, at first glance, more easily cast as broad-gauge social engineers; certainly, their "Puritanism" conveyed a rebuke to the milieu they had left behind. Yet they did *not* see themselves as creators of a new community order. Rather, they sought to restore the shape and tenor of a much older order that most of their contemporaries had seemingly forsaken; they meant, in short, to be heirs of the early Christians. They lamented what they called "evil and declining times" in the land of their birth, but regularly affirmed their connection to it. Indeed, Governor John Winthrop and other leaders of the first settlement at Boston strenuously disavowed any motive of separatism. England remained for them "our native-country [from which] we cannot part without much sadness of heart"; the English church, for all its failings, remained "our dear mother." A bit to their south, in the "Old Colony" at Plymouth, Governor William Bradford claimed that he and his fellow "pilgrims" had left their homeland for "weighty and solid reasons . . . and not out of any newfangledness, or other suchlike giddy humor, by which men are oftentimes transported to their great hurt and danger."[3]

"Newfangledness, or other such-like giddy humors": the pejorative tone is unmistakable. This, in turn, reflected a widespread premodern attitude. "Innovation," for example, was a favorite term of insult, which Puritans in Old England and their religious opponents regularly flung back and forth at one another. And Puritans across the ocean followed suit. Listen to Boston's own Cotton Mather, writing in his diary of one particular local dispute: "I see *Satan* beginning a terrible shake unto the churches of New England; and the *innovators* that have set up a *new* church in Boston (a new one indeed!) have made a day of *temptation* among us."[4] Note the four words that Mather underscored: Satan, temptation, innovators, and new. Evidently, he saw an equivalence among them.

Significantly, too, colonial place-names replicated those of the mother country—by the hundreds. Some embraced entire provinces: New Jersey, New York, New Hampshire. Some were applied to counties: for example, Middlesex, a county name found in three different colonies. And numerous others were for local communities: Boston, Chelsea, Cambridge, Malden, Winchester, Billerica, Reading, Sudbury, Framingham, Dedham, Braintree, Weymouth—to consider only one piece of the initial settlement area (in Massachusetts) with a radius of no more than 15 miles. The qualifier "new," when part of a place-name, was obviously not pejorative, but neither was it distinctive: New England meant (roughly) another edition of the old one—more recent, but of similar design. Nor did these efforts of naming proceed in a vacuum. There were Indian names everywhere, which the colonists occasionally retained but mostly set aside. Agawam became Ipswich; Acushnet became Dartmouth; Winnacunnet became Hampton; and so on. Thus did the settlers (as one of their own historians put it) "imprint some remembrance of their former habitations in England upon their new dwellings in America."

Naming was but the most precise sign of a mass transfer of culture. The tendency to follow traditional English practice was evident in many sectors of colonial life: in land use, home construction, and the "ancient mysteries" of craft production; in foods consumed, in clothes worn, in books read, in words spoken, and in too much else to be noticed here. Of course, the process was not always the same; and the goal was not everywhere realized to an equivalent degree. Houses were smaller, at least for the first generation or two; and maize (Indian corn) was grown in more and more of the freshly cultivated fields. Indeed, in some areas—Virginia, for example—the pattern of material life diverged dramatically from Old World norms. But these were never wished-for developments. In all the colonies, the preferred ways remained English ways. And in some of them preference closely matched reality. Thus was Massachusetts described, twenty years after its founding, as having "become a second England . . . in so short a space [of time] that it is indeed the wonder of the world."[5]

The point of all this is simple, but important. The settlers of America did not mean to be "originators." They sought, insofar as they could, to block out the strangeness of their circumstances—to avoid the pitfalls of "innovation"—to create a "second England." When the country was most profoundly new, the people involved did not—*would* not—recognize it.

The first generation of settlers died without ever recognizing it. But their children, and more especially their children's children, did recognize it—and came to stand in awe of it. The manner of this change is complex and implicates some of the deepest dynamics of early American development, but the result is quite clear. Within a scant few decades of the beginning of settlement, colonists began to look back on it as a transcendently important time. The pattern was clearest in New England, where the image of the "founders"—sometimes they said "forefathers"—became larger and brighter with every passing year. (The linguistic details are themselves suggestive. The old term "settlers" seems modest enough; but both "founders" and "forefathers" have an undertone of grandiloquence.)

Indeed, the New Englanders fashioned an elaborate sense of their own history around this outsized image. The key was what they called "declension"—a process of inner decay after glorious beginnings.[6] Cotton Mather's masterwork, the *Magnalia Christi Americana,* written at the very end of the seventeenth century, makes an excellent case in point. "I write of the wonders of Christian religion, flying from the depravations of Europe, to the American strand": thus Mather's famous opening line (paraphrasing Virgil). Settlement—or "foundation work," as Mather elsewhere called it—was itself a "wonder," beginning with a specific act of "flight" from Old World contamination. The founders were "stars of the first magnitude in our heavens"; and the bulk of the *Magnalia,* presented as a series of biographies, would presumably "immortalize" their deeds. Its basic purpose was nothing less than the following:

> that the true original and design of this plantation may not be lost . . . but [may be] known and remembered forever . . . ; that the names of such eminent persons as

the Lord made use of . . . for the beginning and carrying out of this work . . . may be embalmed and preserved for . . . posterity . . . ; that this present history may stand as a monument, in relation to future time, of a fuller and better reformation of the church of God than hath yet appeared in the world.[7]

Here were joined two ideas that subsequently penetrated to the very marrow of American consciousness: special and sainted origins, and hope for a glorious, even millennial, future.

Perhaps one might suspect Mather and his clergyman colleagues of exaggerating such themes, in the service of their particular goals. But there is evidence of the same way of thinking among humbler folk as well. Consider a few short paragraphs in a stray letter from seventeenth-century Connecticut. (It *is* a stray, but it's also a rare and valuable find.) The writer had been present, as a small child, at the founding of the town of Wethersfield; now he recalled that period, from sixty years later on, for the benefit of his children and grandchildren.

My reverend father was an ordained minister of the Gospel, educated at Cambridge in England, and came to this land by reason of the great persecution . . . I do well remember the face and figure of my honored father. He was 5 foot, 10 inches tall, and spare of build, though not lean. He was as active as the Redskin men, and sinewy. His delight was in sports of strength, and with his own hands he did help to rear both our own house and the first meeting-house of Wethersfield. He was well-featured and fresh-favored with fair skin and long curling hair, with a merry eye and sweet-smiling mouth, though he could frown sternly enough when need was. . . .

The first meeting-house was solid made to withstand the wicked onslaughts of the Redskins. Its foundation was laid in the fear of the Lord, but its walls was truly laid in the fear of the Indians, for many and great was the terrors of 'em.

After the Redskins the great terror of our lives . . . was the wolves. Catamounts were bad enough, and so was the bears, but it was the wolves that was the worst. My mother and sister did each of them kill more than one of the gray howlers, and once my sister shot a bear that came too near the house.[8]

Already the founders—including this letter-writer's parents—are seen through a haze of idealization. And by the early eighteenth century the pattern had become a virtual ancestor worship. Here are two more small examples. The famous Boston magistrate, Samuel Sewall, noted in his (also famous) diary, during the spring of 1726: "The honored, ancient, elder Faunce . . . kindly visited me. Praise God." Thomas Faunce, to whom this comment referred, was then about 80 and had served for many years as deacon of the first church at Plymouth. He was said to have "kept in cherished remembrance the first settlers, many of whom he knew well. He used to point out the rock on which they landed." (Presumably, this was "Pilgrim Rock," the same one that can still be visited at Plymouth today.) Consider, too, a certain Anne Pollard, the subject of a fine portrait painted in 1721 on the occasion of her one-hundredth birthday. (The portrait now has a place of honor in the Massachusetts Historical Society; see Figure 5.) Goodwife Pollard had sailed to Boston with the Winthrop group and had then been the first one off the boat—a spry girl of nine, boldly leading her elders ashore. Or so she claimed, as part of a story that eighteenth-century Bostonians loved to hear retold. To see, and to talk with, the founders (or their friends) was to touch greatness. Life was made brighter—was magnified—as a result.[9]

To recapitulate: by the early eighteenth century the origins of colonial American history were bathed in a kind of rose-tinted spotlight. So what had changed—and why? The first generation of settlers, as noted already, tried mightily to avoid seeing the immensity, the strangeness, the *novelty* of what they were doing. But those who came after them could not help seeing. Central to their perception was the success of the "founders" and "forefathers" in subduing the wilderness and creating human communities seemingly from nothing. The land had become a "pleasant garden": this metaphor, rich in Biblical resonance and endlessly repeated throughout colonial America, became a kind of pushbutton with which later generations might instantly summon their feelings about the founders. Feelings of admiration, verging on awe; feelings of pride and self-enhancement; some feelings, too, perhaps, of envy and at least occasional resentment. It was wonderful to be connected to such magnificent "progenitors" (another favorite term), but impossible to live up to them.

5. Anne Pollard, 1721 (courtesy of the Massachusetts Historical Society).

Let us leap ahead now to the American Revolution, and an era that was to produce a second set of founding fathers. For anyone who has spent a lot of time studying the settlement period, there is—in this later sequence of events—a curious sense of *deja vu.* The people at the center expressed a certain reluctance to see and to admit what they were really about. They repeatedly protested their affection for the "mother-country," even as they loosened the ties that bound them to her. They were not, they said, attempting anything radically new and different, but were simply reacting to recent "tyranny" and reasserting age-old principles of life, liberty, and human happiness. Indeed, a full half-century after the event, Thomas Jefferson would decline to credit the Declaration of Independence with much true "originality." In an 1825 letter to his friend Henry Lee, Jefferson offered this somewhat laconic reflection. The Declaration was meant "not to find new principles, or new arguments, never before thought of, not merely to say things which had never been said before; but to place before mankind the common sense of the subject."[10] The word "merely" seems especially noteworthy here—suggesting, as it does, that received wisdom and "common sense" outweighed the creation of anything genuinely "new." Thus did a little dollop of Bradford's distaste for "giddy . . . newfangledness" survive, even in one of Revolutionary America's most creative leaders.

Yet it would be easy to push such parallels too far. When one reads a little below the surface of the usual Revolutionary rhetoric—which is, of course, where scholars have been reading it for the past generation or two—one comes upon a cross-current that balances old and new in a very different way. The colonists, it is now clear, had become uncomfortable with an imperial regime grown "corrupt," "decadent," flabby—which was almost to say, *old*.[11] In fact, they did not directly say old (at least not very much), but evidently this was part of what they meant. Moreover, when they harked back to the supposedly halcyon conditions of the past, they were actually invoking a time when the colonies were young, and fresh, and *new*. And when they sought to represent their cause in symbolic terms, they famously chose the metaphor of family, and cast themselves as children.[12] Thus, for example, a patriot political leader—none other than John Adams—would repeatedly describe the Revolution as a "vigorous youth." And a patriot political cartoon (one of many such) entitled "Poor England Endeavoring to Reclaim His American Children" depicts a scowling, hawk-nosed, one-legged, and very elderly gentleman, pulling on a cluster of leading-strings attached to a group of unwilling boys.[13] And patriot political organizations reflected the same tendency in the names they gave themselves: Sons of Liberty, Liberty Boys, and so on. In one respect the situation now was entirely different from what had faced the first set of founders; and the difference was precisely that the first set had been there before. The Revolutionaries were trying to renew contact with their own hallowed origins—trying to recover old ways that (nonetheless) epitomized newness, by repudiating new trends that were (in a sense) old.

If that sounds like a muddle—or maybe just a mess—one might well say that it's the way history too often works. In any case, this particular muddle was cleared by many developments immediately subsequent to the Revolution. Then, for the first time, was newness embraced, and celebrated, in quite unequivocal terms. Indeed, the trend seems to have been under way during the war years themselves—witness, for example, such breathless declarations as the following by Thomas Paine (in his enormously influential pamphlet *Common Sense*): "We have it in our power to begin the world over again. A situation similar to the present has not happened since the days of Noah till now. The birth of a new world is at hand." Remember, too, the perennial textbook favorite, taken from Hector St. Jean Crevecoeur's *Letters from an American Farmer:* "What, then, is the American, this new man? He is one who, leaving behind him all his ancient prejudices and manners, receives new ones from the new mode of life he has embraced. He is arrived on a new continent . . . He acts upon new principles; he must therefore entertain new ideas and form new opinions."[14] New, new, new, new: the melody is impossible to miss. And it rises to a powerful crescendo in the years of the early republic (or, for that matter, of the new nation). This extraordinary preoccupation with novelty is well known; we can just replay a few of its most characteristic bars.

The new nation must have a new language. Perhaps English should be abandoned altogether, in favor of Hebrew, or Greek, or some amalgam of Indian tongues. Such extreme possibilities were mentioned in public, though not widely taken up. Piecemeal reform looked more promising (and practical); Noah Webster (of dictionary fame) rose to the task. Take spelling reform, for example; words like "honour," "humour," and "colour" could be Americanized simply be deleting the traditional vowel "u." From such modest beginnings, according to Webster, would come "in the course of time a language in North America as different from the future language of England as the modern Dutch, Spanish, and Swedish are from the German or from each other."[15]

The new nation must have a new system of law. This, too, was hard to work out all at once, since the English common-law tradition was so deeply threaded into the cultural experience of early America. But there were grounds for confidence about the long run. One by one, old precedents and principles might be discarded, or at least revised, so as to conform to republican virtue. "For the western world," wrote one authority, "new and rich discoveries in jurisprudence have surely been reserved."

The new nation must have, if not an entirely new religion, at least a new climate of religious experience. Established churches—that is, churches protected and maintained by state authority—would be no more. The exercise of religious belief must henceforth be voluntary, pluralistic, competitive. Indeed, while the old churches would survive and even prosper under these altered circumstances, there arose new churches as well, in bewildering variety: Moravians, Dunkers, Amish, New Israelites, Followers of the Publick Universal Friend, Millerites, Adventists, Swedenborgians, and (a bit later) the two largest, most quintessentially American of all the new sects, Mormons and Christian Scientists.

The new nation must also have new art forms, a new literature, even a new science. We can safely bypass additional, specific details; but in all these areas there were manifestoes galore, and at least a modest level of accomplishment. And one more thing (if it's not already clear): new was not only necessary, new was also indisputably *better.* Here is a final bit of patriotic effulgence—from a certain Estwick Evans, author of a popular travel book on the "Western territories" published in 1818: "How wonderfully impressive is the prospect, which this country represents to the politician during his cogitation on . . . remote destinies! Everything is conspiring to render the United States far more populous than Europe. In the course of a few hundred years all that is great and splendid will characterize us—the arts of Greece, the arms of Rome, the pride of England will be ours. May God avert the rest!"[16]

One might well observe of this prediction that novelty was not as yet the exclusive focus of American consciousness. The arts of Greece, the arms of Rome, the pride of England: all had long histories of their own. Apparently, some elements of "old" experience might reasonably, and selectively, be appropriated for inclusion in the life of America. But the pattern as a whole would be different from anything known before—would be different, would be better, would be *new*.

So much for our single thread. It's been something of a tangent, perhaps, but the connection to "circles and lines" is important. Baldly put, the point is that their inability—or, indeed, their unwillingness—to come to terms with *novelty* constituted a kind of block, for colonial Americans, against loosening the hold of their very traditional, and fundamentally cyclical, frame of reference.

But, in fact, as and when they reached this point, change —newness, "origination"—was already present around them, in many sectors of their common experience. The eighteenth century was nothing if not a time of sweeping transformation. The historian Jon Butler has recently published an excellent book on this subject entitled *Becoming America: The Revolution before 1776.*[17] The book pulls together all the leading elements of transformation: rapid population growth (and astonishing demographic heterogeneity, too); the movement toward a market economy (with its many attendant elaborations in material life); the evolution of a different (more contentious and popular) style of politics; the advent of a consumer revolution (as many scholars are now calling it); a reorganizing, and diversifying, of organized religion (we've already touched on that one here); and so on. In the Butler argument, "becoming America" is also a process of "becoming modern." And, on the whole, we can embrace it with enthusiasm and real appreciation; in fact, it saves us a lot of effort right now. If anything, we might just underscore it and then ground it somewhat by considering how these broad trends—these large groups, these deep historical forces—can finally be reduced to individual lives and the details of personal experience.

Thus, population growth meant, among other things, that a young man would get squeezed out of the village of his birth—in, for example, coastal New England or tidewater Virginia—where lands were, after a time, fully taken up and opportunity became more and more restricted. He might then head off to some recently opened locale in the "back country" and become a participant—or even a leader —in the creation of a new settlement.

The growth of the market system meant that a small-town artisan—a blacksmith, perhaps—would decide to open a little shop with some retail goods purchased from itinerant peddlers. And when the shop had begun to yield sufficient cash (or credit), he would use it to buy shares in a boat for trading overseas.

The development of a more competitive, popular style of politics meant that in a place like Boston a lumber merchant might decide to stand for election to the town's Board of Assessors. And, if successful, he might become the leader of a lively faction (as they would have called it) devoted to the promotion of the commercial interest (as they also would have called it), and might thus emerge as something of a local power-broker.

The onset of a consumer revolution meant that a well-to-do tobacco planter and his wife—living, say, on Maryland's Eastern Shore—would explore new possibilities for furnishing and decorating their house. (Decorating, to be sure, is our word, not theirs.) A set of country Chippendale chairs, a few prints or even a portrait to hang on the walls, a corner cupboard in which to display some pewter tableware—artifacts, all, of a budding gentility to which they could then impart their own particular style and tone.

We could easily create more such imaginary vignettes, if their overall drift were not already clear. These folk, these eighteenth-century colonial Americans, were agents—doers, "originators"—whether they recognized it or not. But that, again, is the crucial point: mostly, they *didn't* recognize it: didn't want to, didn't know how to, just didn't. They preferred to see themselves as done to, rather than doing—as recipients of God's favor (or, in some cases, of His chastisement), as objects, not subjects, in the flow of history. They continued to search for cues to behavior outside rather than within the self. And in all this, they remained effectively traditional.

Indeed, there is a kind of missing element in Jon Butler's fine account of "becoming America." No part of it deals with mentality—ideas, attitudes, values—in any sustained, head-on way. And this, I suggest, is not an accident, not a mistake either, not even an inadvertent omission; instead, it's an important indicator. Again (baldly and broadly speaking), changes in experience, changes in behavior, came first, while changes in mentality lagged behind—and would not be realized, at least not very much, until after the start of the next (the nineteenth) century. In a certain sense, America became America before Americans became Americans (in the way we've come to think of them). There were exceptions, of course. Some individual lives—whole lives—might be exceptions; Benjamin Franklin's is perhaps the first to come to mind. But the vast majority of eighteenth-century Americans retained their conservative and cyclical mentality, even as their experience began to move in fresher, more linear, channels. To put it back into the framework of our single-thread exploration: they resisted, or at least they averted their eyes from, the novelty that was steadily infusing their lives.

What would finally get them off the dime here? Maybe we could simply say that these things take a while, that the psyche is (in most of us, anyhow) intrinsically conservative—preferring proven ways, and cautious about accepting change. Maybe a few decades, even a generation or two, had to pass before change could be accepted as the norm. In fact, we can easily believe that—up to a point. And it's part of the answer to our question here—up to a point. But there is more. So now we need to ask, front and center: what about the Revolution itself, as a force for counteracting, and undercutting, this aspect of traditional mentality? The link seems immediately plausible, and significant.

We can zero in on that link by considering the *word* revolution and its own history of change. In fact, it's not too much to say that the word moved from an originally circular to an eventually linear meaning, over the span of several centuries. Other scholarly hands have been into this history—of the word—in some detail.[18] Their conclusions deserve a careful summary. Revolution was, during the late Middle Ages and on into the early modern period, used to refer to things that turned, that rotated—circular and cyclical things. (In this it followed the sense of its Latin root.) Most especially was it used by astronomers to describe the orbital movement of the stars—for example, in the landmark work of Copernicus, *De Revolutionibus Orbium Coelestium*. Then bit by bit it was brought down from the heavens and applied to more earthly matters—as a metaphor for revolving tendencies of all sorts. Then, in the seventeenth century, it became a specifically political term, but still with the underlying sense of movement around and back to pre-established positions. This was especially true of its widespread application to political events in England from mid-century onward: the Puritan Revolution (which, from the perspective of many, represented a turning back toward older and better ways), and also the Glorious Revolution of 1688 (which was widely understood as a restoration of monarchical power to its appropriate form and context).

And that was where the meaning of the term remained for quite a while longer—indeed, until the last part of the eighteenth century. The American Revolution, as we've already remarked, was begun in a spirit of restoration, of re-engaging principles and structures supposedly forgotten (or abandoned, or subverted). Thus the word, in its traditional usage, was initially a good fit. But when the political context changed—when the historical actors began to acknowledge, and even to embrace, the novelty of what they were about—the word changed, too. This is the truly remarkable thing: events reversed a meaning that had endured for several hundred years. From now on, revolution would signify not a turning back into old paths but the creation of entirely new ones. (This result was solidified, just a few years further ahead, with the start of the French Revolution. There, too—though perhaps a bit more ambiguously—one sees a movement away from restorative conceptions toward openly innovative ones.)

Moreover, one could argue that the change in meaning not only caught up with but actually ran ahead of the shift in political orientation. Here is an odd, and illustrative, moment in the career of Thomas Paine—he of the "begin-the-world-over-again" comment in *Common Sense*. Some years after this pamphlet was printed, when Paine was debating Edmund Burke on "the rights of man," he wished to associate those rights—and the American Revolution itself—with ancient and honorable tradition. The trouble was that "revolution" had by now assumed its innovative meaning, so Paine felt obliged to propose the term "counter-Revolution" as a way of designating both the American and the French struggles. In short, only by adding the modifier "counter"—and again standing things on their head—could he recapture the original sense of the word as a turning back.[19]

Confusing, isn't it! But, in fact, these very particular dilemmas of Thomas Paine reflected a much larger theme—the way traditional and modern elements were constantly in play, and pitted against one another, within the Revolutionary movement all along. We need to say a little more about this. And in doing so we must somehow distill—in a drastically foreshortened way—a lot of well-known, recent scholarship. The traditional part of the Revolutionary viewpoint, the one that looked mostly back in time toward venerable, classical models, is encapsulated for us now in the term "re-publicanism" (small r). And by "classical" we mean starting with ancient Greece and Rome and carried forward through the Renaissance, the English "Commonwealth," the Glorious Revolution, and the "country-party" opposition in early- to mid-eighteenth-century British politics. These connections, up to and through their importance for the American Revolution, have been powerfully dissected by the (so-called) neo-Whig school of historians: Bernard Bailyn, Gordon Wood, John Pocock, and a host of gifted students and followers. Meanwhile, opposite the neo-Whigs and "republicanism" stands "liberalism"—a very different set of ideas, of which the chief scholarly expositors include, a couple of generations ago, Louis Hartz and, more recently, Joyce Appleby.[20]

The line-up here is familiar, both the players and their various scholarly moves. But what seems particularly important just now is the bearing of this debate on the "circles and lines" theme. Republicanism not only supported a restorative sense of revolution; it also contained at its core a view of politics—the history of politics—as being fundamentally cyclical. The formula was, at bottom: monarchy devolves into tyranny, which presently gives way to aristocracy, which in turn becomes oligarchy, which eventually yields to democracy, which finally sinks into anarchy—which then returns to monarchy, starting the whole process over again. In sum: a long wheel turning; history repeating itself; revolution in the old sense. It was a lot more nuanced than that, as elaborated (and applied to actual situations) both by political theorists in the eighteenth century and by scholars in the twentieth. But its underlying, circular aspect seems clear. Even the most hopeful republicans of Revolutionary America acknowledged the limits this viewpoint implied. How, they wondered, could the eventual decline and death of their political creations be forestalled (postponed, minimized, neutralized)?

Liberalism, by contrast, was fundamentally linear. Its central affirmations—free choice, free inquiry, individual autonomy, rational self-interest—were typically expressed as a *quest:* an unfolding, a moving forward, and (in some versions at least) an idea of progress. Its posture toward history was fashioned accordingly; history appeared not as a storehouse of lessons or models or precedents, but, at most, as a sequence of precursors leading up to an essentially singular present. Thus, too, its orientation to the future. Many Revolutionary leaders displayed a remarkable preoccupation with "posterity," and (as one scholar has put it) "looked at their own conduct through the eyes of the unborn."[21] In short: past, present, and future would *all* be singular.

Both strands were present, influential, and closely entangled—yet quite substantially at odds with one another—in the sequence we know as the American Revolution. It isn't possible to choose between them or even to decide which was more important in making the Revolution go; evidently, the neo-Whig historians have got one large piece of the truth, and their liberalism-minded opponents have got another. But it does seem clear which won out in the long run—in all the years and decades following the Revolution. That was, and is, liberalism; can there really be much doubt? (To be sure, it wasn't a complete victory; we do retain a measure of republican values right up to the present day. But, mostly, liberalism won.)

As to the *reason* liberalism won, we can lift a couple of sentences out of Appleby. "Liberalism," she writes, "offered an openness to change, to a society that was changing without a supportive ideology." Its appeal was especially to such "upwardly mobile" social groups as "tradesmen, mechanics, and newly launched merchants," all of whom epitomized "a new image of human nature, *homo faber*"—that is, the man who works, who makes, who produces. To repeat: "a society that was changing without a supportive ideology."[22] That seems parallel to, if not quite the same as, the argument presented above—about experience moving forward (in eighteenth-century America) while mentality lagged behind, about more and more individuals acting in forceful, sometimes innovative, ways without (as yet) managing to credit their acting for what it truly was.

So this is what it finally comes down to. The gradual, piecemeal, and cumulatively large *social* changes of the early and middle decades of the eighteenth century were followed by a *political* change of corresponding dimensions. The Revolution was *un*precedented, *in*comparable, *ir*reversible —the start of a future that had never previously existed. As it proceeded, its agents and advocates (and, for that matter, its opponents, too) could not avoid seeing its novel essence. The result was a massive shock to the system—in a social, cultural, and psychological sense, as much as the institutional one. Moreover, the process of Revolution-*making* brought traditional and modern orientations into the open—there is a lot of hindsight in the way we use those terms, but for now we have nothing better—and faced them off against each other in a kind of implicit, but thoroughgoing and transformative, contest. And the people who lived through those years and those events were marked—inwardly marked—in unmistakable ways. Put differently: their mentality at last caught up with their experience. And their post-Revolution lives would, as a result, proceed on a new, more linear, and (again, seen in hindsight) distinctively modern track.

But this is just to beg a host of further questions. What we are really asking here is how much—and in what ways, and to what lasting extent—did the Revolution change human psychology? It's one thing to suggest how the traditional and the modern, the cyclical and the linear, met—and clashed—inside the rhetorical top tier of the Revolutionary movement, with its high-flown political theory and such. But it would be quite another thing to show how the same conflicts played out among ordinary folk. (We're aiming, after all, for social history.) We know a great deal, by now, about the political history of the Revolution, and the intellectual history, and even the social history, in what might be called an aggregate sense. But on the other side—the personal, the emotional, the psychological—what have we really got? We've got (from a couple of decades back) some suggestive work about the impulse to patricide—"killing the king," the Revolution as Oedipus—but that seems so very broad and schematic.[23] We've got some thoughtful comparison of the patriot mindset with the motivation behind modern-day "wars of liberation"—the Revolution as Vietnam—but that's an awfully long stretch.[24] We've got some of the neo-Whig historians occasionally invoking the clinical term paranoid—the Revolution as psychopathology—but they mean it only in a quasi-metaphorical sense. What we don't have is any full-scale, frontal treatment of innerlife experience among average people who lived in and through the Revolutionary era. No scholar has even attempted such a project. So what I propose, in concluding the present discussion, is to begin a process of imagining that project—by walking its boundaries, roughing out some of its structural contours, and casting at least a few glances toward its very center.

We can hardly doubt, in the first place, that the start of the Revolution was a profoundly unsettling moment for many of those most directly involved. Unsettling, intense, urgent, anxious: they had a powerful sense of launching out through uncharted territory, with peril at every turn. The enemy was in all ways formidable. And the stakes seemed exceedingly high: "liberty or death," in the conventional formula. Death could, of course, be literal, be physical; and many lives would end in the ensuing struggle. But death could be moral and spiritual as well. Failure to achieve the goal of independence would likely amount to an inward dying—an emptying, a numbing, a deep-down enervation of the soul.

Listen to the way one young Pennsylvania minister described his feelings when preaching on a Continental fast day (July 20, 1775). "I spoke in great Fear and Dread—I was never before so nice an Audience—I never spoke on so solemn a Day—In spite of all my Fortitude and Practice, when I begun, my Lips quivered, my Flesh shrunk, my Hair rose up; my Knees trembled—I was wholly confused till I had almost closed the sermon."[25] We have no record of his auditors' reaction, but it seems safe to assume that they, too, felt the urgency of the moment. We do have additional evidence about preachers—the Revolution's "Black Regiment"—for they left both sermon notes and (in some cases) personal diaries. Their anxiety was, and still is, palpable in such documents. Sleeplessness, loss of appetite, alarming dreams, plus innumerable versions of "Fear and Dread": all were mentioned and linked to their distress. Their sermons, too, showed the burdens they were under. Their rhetorical strategies became less and less coherent, their point of view disoriented, their very language (as another scholar has put it) "unmoored from traditional contexts, referents, and canons of style."[26]

While the war lengthened and deepened, "Americans followed events with extravagant, see-sawing moods. Joy and optimism took turns with gloom as one story or rumor followed another."[27] (This is from Charles Royster's *A Revolutionary People at War,* a work that gets at least somewhat closer than any other to the psychological dimension.) Soldiers and civilians alike continued to invest the entire struggle with cosmic moral significance, and repeatedly questioned the depth and sincerity of their own contributions. The practice of "virtue" would be decisive (according to numerous political and religious leaders). Conversely, "Fear was Treason" (in the words of a widely reprinted newspaper article). Moreover, the interests of "posterity" loomed larger and larger; failure now would mean failure forever.[28]

When it was over—when success, not failure, was certain—they would look back with wonder on all they had endured. The drama, the emotionality, the sheer intensity of it astonished them. Yale president Ezra Stiles commented that "We have lived an age in a few years. We have seen more wonders accomplished in *eight* years than are usually unfolded in a century." A young officer's wife felt that "she *lived* more in one year at this period of excitement than in a dozen of ordinary life." A poet, referring to his own participation in "so great a contest," declared simply "life is redoubled."[29]

But still: how much, and in what ways, were they changed, inwardly *changed*? "Our style and manner of thinking," wrote Paine in 1782, "have undergone a revolution more extraordinary than the political revolution of the country. We see with other eyes; we hear with other ears; and think with other thoughts, than those we formerly used." Paine's wonderful way with words is, in this case, just a tease: *What* "other eyes . . . other ears . . . other thoughts"?[30]

Two separate scholarly currents suggest a way forward. First, a considerable body of recent work, mainly by literature specialists, investigates writers and writing in the immediate post-Revolutionary period.[31] Taken as a whole, it is much too varied and complex for any quick summary; but one important theme can be pried out and presented here. Contingency—the uncertain, unstable, indeterminate conditions of life; the sense, as one minister described it, of being "lost and bewildered in the darkness of the night"—this element appears again and again, in fiction, in autobiography, even in some sermonic writing. Plus the idea (as Stephen Carl Arch has put it) that "personal identity was not and could not be a fixed, known thing." Plus a quite pervasive preoccupation with questions of "representation, authenticity, deception, counterfeiting, [and] causation." In short: things fall apart; experience is not as it appears; identity itself lies in question. May we not see just here—in the recognition, however reluctant and pained, of the power of contingency—a break in the traditional "circle" of experience, and an opening toward more linear ways?[32]

Finally, the deepest, truest gauge of psychological change is always by way of individuals (the innerlife experience of as large and representative a "sample" as possible). And here we come up especially short. There are, to be sure, suggestive fragments. Royster's book includes occasional stories of particular soldiers showing "increased self-respect." One, in protesting to a postwar employer about his conditions of work, "told him that I had ben about the world and in jentlemen's Company." Another, while arguing the case for officers' pensions, declared that "Men by a more free intercourse with the world [through travel with the army, for example] enlarge their understanding and acquire a more liberal way of thinking."[33] Such comments do imply connection between experience of the Revolution and innerlife change. But they would need to be multiplied many times over in order to yield any solid result.

There is one source more to mention: the recently published study by Alfred F. Young of a "common soldier" named George Robert Twelves Hewes. This is, in fact, the only book of its kind—the only substantial biography of an ordinary person in the Revolutionary era. Young addresses many aspects of his subject's life, psychology among them. And his conclusion weighs strongly on the side of change. The gist is that Hewes changed during the course of the war years (beginning, in fact, during the years just before) from a humble lad "tongue-tied in the face of his betters" to "a defiant person who would not take his hat off for any man." He then maintained this assertive stance through the rest of his extremely long life and engaged in repeated efforts of self-invention. Indeed, when fully in his 90s, he managed to cast himself as an important public figure—an erstwhile "hero" of the Boston Tea Party and other Revolution-related engagements.[34]

Young's work on Hewes is, as noted, one of a kind. But the possibilities are there for a great deal more. Young notes the existence of at least 500 first-person accounts by and about war veterans (memoirs, newspaper articles, "narratives," all dating from the period). And there are pension records (often including much biographical detail) for many others. Someday, one hopes, this material will be mined for that project we don't (yet) have: a full-fledged psychological history of the American Revolution. Until it happens, we cannot finally trace the movement from cyclical to linear, through what was evidently its crucial phase.

We do have a better fix on where things came out—after the Revolution, in the age of the new nation. And that's what we'll turn to next.

3

The Modern World and
the Rise of the Linear

Perhaps we should back up, and give ourselves a kind of running start for this final discussion, by briefly recapping the previous two. In the first, the gist was all the different dimensions of early American, premodern, "cyclical" experience: their embeddedness in the various rhythms of Nature (capital N), and at least some of their links to various aspects of culture (broadly construed). In the second, we sought to explore how, mainly in the eighteenth century, these folk began to break out and move toward a more "linear" orientation. In that connection, our focus became changing attitudes toward novelty and newness, especially at two key historical junctures: settlement, in the early to mid-seventeenth century, and the run-up to (and through) the American Revolution, in the late eighteenth.

There is more to say about this pair of pregnant moments. With settlement, novelty was essentially—even willfully and massively—denied. But with the Revolution, it was—after some ambiguity and waffling—embraced. So the question then follows: why the difference between these two patterns of reaction? Certainly, it helped in the second case to have the first one behind (chronologically behind). It also helped that considerably before the Revolution a process of broad-gauge social, economic, and cultural change was well under way. But there is one additional point to add now, and it relates more to the first than to the second of these novelty-laden sequences.

The word "settlement" has such a nice, comfortable sound; the experience, of course, was anything *but* comfortable. This seems obvious enough; yet early American historians have not, on the whole, done justice to the discomforts of settlement. Indeed, "discomforts" seems a grossly inadequate term for describing what was involved here. I hadn't myself taken all this in until obliged to do so by the work of Kathleen Donegan. Donegan argues for a hugely traumatic underside in, and all through, the settlement process—and she borrows somewhat the actual clinical concept of "trauma" to make her case.[1]

Donegan's work (a nearly completed dissertation) offers fresh readings of well-known, indeed altogether famous, texts from the period: for example, William Bradford's history *Of Plimoth Plantation*. If we open our eyes—and our brain, and our empathy—enough, *Plimoth Plantation* appears as a fundamentally mournful document, with the pain of loss and dislocation at its core. And there are others like it. The point is that—given the deeply traumatic nature of the settlement process—an impulse of conservatism, of clinging to whatever could be saved from old patterns and values was, in the fullest sense, necessary. Novelty, in that context, could be experienced only in the most downside way. (Better, in fact, not to experience it at all.) In short: if novelty and innovation were already, within premodern culture, highly suspect categories, this attitude would become intensified—and locked into place—for the settlement generation by their unsettling experiences.

With the Revolutionary generation, however, the situation was different. For them, novelty—innovation, change—would increasingly mean *liberation;* thus it took hold, as it never could have done with their immigrant ancestors. We don't, by the way, commonly apply the term "immigrant" to the settlement cohort; we reserve it for a later part of American history. But immigrants they surely were. One is reminded, with regard to the "trauma" angle here, of Oscar Handlin's classic study of nineteenth- and twentieth-century immigration, the book he called *The Uprooted.* That metaphor works just as well for the seventeenth century; maybe, in fact, it works even better.[2]

We must fast-forward now across several generations into the early nineteenth century. The Revolution is in our rearview mirror and fading out of sight; and a great deal looks different. Indeed, we can see linear ways of acting, linear ways of thinking, linear ways of *being,* in every direction. The problem is where to put the focus, how to break into this new landscape, which appears (from a distance anyway) so integrated—so virtually seamless—as a whole? My own instinct, when faced with such difficulties, is to start with individuals and their particular life stories. Therefore we're going to focus next on personal documents: how they changed their look as time moved along. And not just their look, but also their purposes, their content and context, their cadence and tone. (To do this right, we'll actually have to *use* the rearview mirror again—at least a certain amount—for the sake of comparison and contrast.)

We can start with some brief consideration of diaries and diary-keeping.[3] In the premodern period, up until around 1750, American diaries were of three main sorts. The first was for the purpose of spiritual self-examination; this, as anyone might imagine, was characteristic of Puritans (in New England and elsewhere) and especially of Puritan ministers. The substance, as one would also imagine, was lots of heavily introverted comment—very private, but also somewhat formulaic—full of confession, and regret, and resolution to do better. It's a genre that fits, in obvious ways, with much else in the religious culture of the period (again, especially "Puritan" religious culture); but there is no need now to draw out all those links. A second type of early American diary involved the factual recording of particular secular events—especially work-related events, and family events—in the life of the keeper. Small business transactions; the performance of seasonal chores; weather notations; personal illnesses; the comings and goings of friends and neighbors: thus the usual content, often put down in a very telegraphic style, and with not much more than a line or two per day (and not every day either). The overall effect, at least for a reader two or three hundred years later on, is pretty sparse and repetitive; you have to grit your teeth and resolve to keep going in order to get anything much out of such material. The third diary type to mention here was essentially a record of "providences." We touched on the theme of providences in Chapter 1: moments, and events, that seemed way out of the ordinary—and were considered "remarkable" precisely because they interrupted the regular, cyclical rhythms of experience, and thus seemed likely to disclose some purpose of the Almighty. For the same reason, they would be taken as things very much worth pondering, remembering, and making a diary about.

They are quite different from one another, these three types. But, setting difference aside, we can register a few general impressions that apply to them all. When one reads them, one gets precious little sense of the individuals who wrote them; or, to put it differently, there is no "personality" in them. (This is the reason most of us wouldn't particularly enjoy spending a lot of time with them; by our lights, they're boring!) Another point, too: they seem, in effect, to lack any clear element of motion. Their sometimes numerous bits and pieces don't really go anywhere, or even connect in meaningful ways. They come across as essentially a list—whether of sins and penances, or of practical details, or indeed of providences; whichever the type, they don't tell a story.

Now, it may sound not only ungenerous, but also ahistorical, to emphasize what these early American diaries seem *not* to offer. Except that, when we turn to diary-keeping in the nineteenth century, this is exactly what does begin to appear: individual personality, on the one hand, and cumulative connection, on the other. People increasingly write them*selves* onto the page, and those selves, in turn, stretch nicely from one entry to the next. This is achieved partly by the inclusion, more and more, of affective experience (feelings of pride, pleasure, disappointment, distress, and so on). And partly, too, it reflects an increasing tendency to cross-reference—that is, to look back from whatever is the present moment to the past, or forward to the future. The sense of it, then, is *not* a list, but rather a line, or even a narrative.

In the first chapter we gave passing notice also to almanacs as an especially important print form in early America; it will be useful now to bring almanacs back for another brief turn. An almanac, of course, was essentially a calendar, with lots of astronomical information attached to its various parts, and lots of practical, farm-related information, too. As such, it was intrinsically circular in its arrangements. It reflected, in fact, elements of three different circular rhythms, all firmly grounded in Nature: the diurnal one (sunrise and sunset times), the lunar one (the waxing and waning of the moon), and finally the seasonal one. Yet, as time passed, almanacs became blended with diary-keeping, because individuals began to use them to record personal information alongside the printed dates; sometimes they did this by quite literally writing between the lines. Then, after a little more time passed, almanac makers (and printers) decided to include special blank pages for this purpose—set right into the middle of the printed monthly calendars— thereby inviting their use as diaries. Such juxtaposition of broad, environmental rhythms, which were the same for everyone, with the ongoing record of a single life, unique at least in detail, serves to epitomize a transitional phase in the circles-to-lines sequence.[4]

There is another kind of text to consider here: autobiographies. Again, we can start by looking back to the colonial period. And in so doing, we can bring onstage a specific, entirely ordinary character from early American history: a man named John Dane, who was born in England, the son of a tailor, around the year 1612; who was himself trained as a tailor in his father's shop; who emigrated to Massachusetts about 1640; who settled in the town of Ipswich on the North Shore, where he lived—mainly as a farmer—for many subsequent years. Shortly before his death in 1684, John Dane composed a kind of memoir which he called "A Declaration of Remarkable Providences in the Course of My Life."[5] The title is a tipoff to the contents of this very characteristic, very Puritan, very premodern document. Notice right away that it doesn't say (some version of) "myself and my story"; instead, it's about "remarkable providences," amazing and noteworthy things that happened to me, and around me, while I was alive. (There's a difference—and it's significant.)

Looking into the document itself, one finds it arranged in roughly chronological order—but only *very* roughly, with long gaps between the various "providences," and virtually no specific time notation at all. Moreover, it's a list, a collection—A, B, C, D—the lucky finding of some valuable coins at a time when the family was destitute; narrowly averting seduction (several times) as a young man; a seemingly miraculous recovery from illness; the decision to migrate to New England on the basis of a "sign" found in the Bible; a devastating house fire—all presented with the aim of proving the same point about God's "over-arching rule." In short: as is true also of the early diaries, there is no movement here, no cumulative feeling of growth and change, and not much of the writer in it either; it would provide no good basis for picking John Dane out of a crowd.

Dane's "Declaration" was apparently intended for the private use of his "loving relations" (descendants). And the same was true of other autobiographical writings from the colonial era. Thus, the Puritan poet Anne Bradstreet addressed "to My Dear Children" a declaration of her own, in which events from her life were selectively presented "not to set forth myself, but the glory of God . . . [in order that] you may gain some spiritual advantage by my experience." And the Reverend Thomas Shepard (first minister to the congregation at Cambridge, Massachusetts) composed a similar document, with "records of God's great kindness to him," for the direct benefit of "my deare son."[6]

Now jump ahead 150 years and see how much the prospect—the autobiographical prospect—has changed.[7] First comes the matter of quantity, the sheer number of such writings that got produced (starting in the early-to-mid nineteenth century) and in many cases (even quite humble cases) put into print. There was on all sides a spreading urge to tell one's life story.[8] Presumably, too, there was hope for an interested audience of some sort. But it's evident overall how much these people, these autobiographers, were writing for their own benefit; they rather enjoyed the sound of their own voices (or at least the look of their own prose). One could say, standing back a bit, that in composing their life stories they were defining themselves—or, to use a bit of currently voguish scholars' lingo, that such autobiographical ventures were part of a project of "self-fashioning." The contrast to Dane, Bradstreet, Shepard, and other seventeenth-century autobiographers could hardly be greater. For this much earlier group, "self" was decidedly *off* center; instead, their center—as writers—was all the unusual things they had witnessed and endured, the "providences" that revealed the will of God.

There is a fundamental connection here that is, admittedly, a little hard to nail down. In some deep way, a sharper sense of self—a stronger articulation of self—accompanied the development of a linear mode of experience. And, to be sure, the business of more and more self-*hood,* including the kind of self-fashioning to which we've just referred—all this has been a mainstay of recent scholarship about the transition from premodern to modern culture.[9] Whether a strongly articulated self is a prerequisite for linear living, or the other way around, seems impossible to say. Most likely, this is another unfathomable chicken-and-egg linkage; the two aspects just seemed to proceed together, in a mutually reinforcing way.

The nineteenth-century autobiographies are worth our further—still closer—attention. They have a very clear, sharp, indeed linear structure. They go from a beginning, through a middle (sometimes a long and tortuous middle), to an end. The beginnings seem especially striking—for example, this one from the autobiography of John Ball, a pioneer businessman (and public figure) in Michigan during the early and middle decades of the century. "Now back to the time of my birth, let me look at the state and condition of the world": thus his opening sentence. Ball goes on to set that stage with a summary of national (and international) developments in the immediate post-Revolution years; he also provides a little family history (genealogy). Then: "here on this bleak high hill was I born, the tenth child of my parents."[10] In effect, he creates a kind of double beginning—one at a fairly global level, the other, quite personal and specific. Together they establish a very firm starting-point from which all else will then proceed. John Dane's "Declaration"—to invoke that contrast once again—had begun: "And I speak first of a family providence . . . " In short, Dane just launched into the list, saying nothing at all about his birth or the condition of the world; indeed, it's not even clear how old he was when a first "family providence" occurred.

The nineteenth-century autobiographies also feature another kind of beginning, linked to the time of leaving home (the home, that is, of the writer's birth family). Sometimes this is presented as a triumphant moment, with no regrets attached. Thus, for example, Chester Harding, who would go on to become a painter of considerable note, wrote of his own leave-taking: "I launched forth into the wide world in pursuit of fortune." Sometimes it appears as a heart-rending scene—as, for instance, in the case of a clockmaker named Chauncey Jerome: "Never shall I forget the Monday morning [he even remembers the day of the week] that I took my little bundle of clothes and with a bursting heart bid my poor mother goodbye." Sometimes it seems affectively neutral but still momentous; thus Daniel Drake, a Kentucky doctor, spoke of it as a "governing event," one with consequences "ranging far up and down the chronography of my life."[11] (The word "chronography" is a nice touch, especially for its linear connotations.)

The middle parts of these autobiographical writings are, typically, a succession of adventurous "scenes" and "incidents." (Incidents was a favorite period word, with a meaning very different from "providences.") Put together, they serve to plot "the current of my life," or "a broad highway," or simply "a journey"; the language of movement and of travel is recurrent and revealing. Often enough, moreover, there is a sense of *upward* movement, of leaving former positions behind and below; but we should note, too, that many autobiographers acknowledged setbacks and disappointments along the way (business failures, for example). Thus the life-*lines* we are following here were never entirely straight; to the contrary, they usually had something of a zig-zag quality. One writer produced an especially arresting image of all this when he commented that "human life itself is but one long and large tangled skein."[12]

Still, the key thing was, and is, that they came out in a very different place from wherever it was they had started. And virtually *all* nineteenth-century autobiographers feature the aspect of change—both change they had experienced and witnessed and, in at least some cases, change they had personally caused. Indeed, this element could scarcely be overemphasized. Thus, "What a great change has taken place in so short a space of time." Or, "Everyday things with us now would have appeared to our forefathers as incredible." Sometimes, too, a writer would declare how unexpected—and impossible to predict—were the nature and amount of the changes involved. For instance: "I little thought then that I should ever live there [referring to New Haven] with three hundred men in my employ." (That was the clockmaker, a man who became hugely successful.)[13] In short, one sees no circling back here to old and familiar positions; instead, experience marches ever *forward,* toward who-knows-what future destinations. One might even speak of a characteristic "future orientation" running all through these writings. Listen to the way the aforementioned Dr. Drake (of Kentucky) recalled the moment of his marriage: "It was all before us, and we were under the influence of the same ambition to possess it: to acquire not wealth merely, but friends, knowledge, influence, distinction."[14] To repeat, "it was all before us"—it, presumably, meaning the rest of Life. One could hardly imagine a better way to epitomize the spirit of this entire autobiographical corpus.

And there are still *more* things to notice about it; for example, a pervasive attitude of planfulness and preparation (even as the writers admitted their inability to predict what was coming next). Thus, education assumed a special importance—in some cases, formal schooling (at one or another academy or college); in others, a process of self-tuition. Here is a woman autobiographer describing part of her life as a newlywed:

> We commenced immediately after our marriage a system of study, which we pursued together, with few interruptions . . . The hours we allotted for this purpose were from eight o'clock in the evening till ten. In this manner we studied French, botany—then almost a new science in this country—but for which my husband had an uncommon taste—and obtained some knowledge of mineralogy, geology, chemistry, besides pursuing a long and instructive course of miscellaneous reading.[15]

It seems notable, too, that they viewed education as a continuing, and never-ending, process. One man, recalling his student days at Dartmouth, included this comment by the college president: "You must still be pupils all your lives."[16] Another aspect of "future orientation" was their belief that education involved more than mastering a set body of traditional wisdom; instead, it would unfold in new and sometimes surprising channels, just as life unfolds, piece by piece and year after year.

One could compile a list of keywords from this literature: "opportunity" (that's everywhere), "striving," "exertion," "ambition." We should pause for a moment over "ambition" and its own history of change. Briefly summarized, ambition was a bad word, a bad *thing,* in premodern times—full of potential danger and disruption. But then came a major reversal that yielded a much more positive evaluation, beginning around the year 1800.[17]

Finally, we need to say a bit more about the affective side—the emotional tone—of the autobiographies. On the whole, they have a sort of breathless quality: eyes bulging, heart pumping, brain churning, and so on. Some quick examples would be: "I was more and more astonished at the wonderful things that I saw." And, "I asked what all this excitement meant." And, "Imagine my amazement when . . ."[18] The late psychologist Silvan Tomkins, a leader in the scientific study of affect, proposed a fundamental distinction between cultures that especially value "enjoyment" and others that prize "excitement."[19] Measured against this typology, the nineteenth-century autobiographies tilt heavily toward excitement—a tendency that does seem to reflect their linear predisposition. Conversely, one might speculate that the circular, and cyclical, mode fits well with a posture of enjoyment.

This two-part contrast, the seventeenth versus the nineteenth century, raises obvious questions about what came in-between. How were autobiographical writers operating in the years just before, during, and after the American Revolution? In fact, as Stephen Carl Arch has shown in an excellent new investigation of exactly that period, the entire genre was passing through a fundamental and "many-stranded" transition. Arch points out that the word "autobiography" does not appear before 1780 and was not used in any book title before about 1830. These nominative facts undergird his decision to reserve it for writings that conformed to an elaborate set of "modern" criteria—in contrast to what he calls the "self-narratives" of the premodern era. The criteria include a focus on private, interior experience; a feeling of "independence"; an acceptance of originality and individual uniqueness; an acknowledgment of personal agency and ambition; an embracing of the goal of "invention." During the crucial fifty-year transitional period, particular self-narratives expressed these elements in differing —but steadily accumulating—ways.[20]

Benjamin Franklin's *History of My Life,* the most famous of all American autobiographical writings, can stand as a case in point. In some ways it exemplified the evolving modern pattern—witness its forward, future-directed outlook; its connected and cumulative sense of experience; the self firmly situated at its center; and so on. In other ways, however, it remained effectively traditional. Thus the "self" in question was more social (and patterned) than separate (and individualized), more a product of "imitation" and "emulation" (Arch's terms) than of original "invention."[21] And so, too, with other roughly contemporaneous, if less well-known, autobiographical accounts; indeed, the range of their permutations and combinations became remarkably wide.

Eventually, by or before mid-century, the various new elements coalesced to create the modern form of autobiography. And this, in turn, gave expression to an idea, and a word, that was itself dramatically changing—namely, "career." Actually, the word goes back to at least the sixteenth century, when, however, its principal meaning was a race course (for horses). Sometimes, too, it could refer to the act of racing—a horse running at a gallop. Part of that original meaning is retained today in the verb form—to career. But as of about 1800, the noun shifted from horses to people and from sport to life experience (especially work experience). No doubt there was a metaphorical piece that facilitated this transfer: life itself as a race, a gallop, a rapid, action-packed sequence extending from a starting line to a finishing tape. Only within the past several decades has a further evolution taken place, from which career has come to mean a particular type, or area, of work.[22]

In the nineteenth century the word still had, at its core, the element of motion; hence its link to the autobiographical accounts. For, again, autobiographies became, above all, stories of motion, of tacking here and there and hardly ever remaining in the same place for more than a few moments. We shouldn't imagine, however, that the careers in question followed a consistent track, such as a single line of work. (That would take it closer to the present-day meaning: a legal career, a teaching career.) Instead, nineteenth-century careers often involved a fitful process of stitching together different kinds of work for intervals of several years apiece. But the point is that somehow, in the end, they did add up—did roughly cohere, did follow a "course," however ragged its specific parts.

From career we need to make a quick switch back to the life cycle, on which we reflected at some length in the first of these discussions. Recall, then, its major features within the colonial American setting: the fuzziness of its parts, its incompleteness (especially considering the absence of any clearly articulated midlife stage), its essentially circular shape. By the nineteenth century, much of this was changing. For one thing, there was a new and special concentration on the opening phases of the life cycle. Childhood came to seem particularly distinct—not just a stage but a "status" or even a "condition."[23]

This change was rooted in the long transition from a rural, farm-based mode of living (characteristic of all premodern society) to the urban, commercial/industrial mode of the succeeding period. Crudely put, the point is that children, even quite young children, had traditionally been drawn into the work life of their farm families, contributing in small ways to household production and gradually learning, through a quite informal process of apprenticeship, the work routines and responsibilities they would one day assume as adults. For that matter, something similar was true of regular craft apprentices in premodern communities: they, too, started young, learned gradually, and ended up as facsimiles of their masters (or parents). The growth sequence, in nearly all cases, was evenly paced, gradual, seamless. And its terminus, its goal, was tangibly embodied in the form of the adults, especially the same-sex adults, to whom the child was most closely connected: little boys modeled on their fathers, little girls on their mothers.

But move away from the farm—go to Boston, New York, Cincinnati, St. Louis, or any other of the rapidly burgeoning nineteenth-century cities—and the entire landscape of childhood seems transformed. Especially in the (so-called) middle class and upward on the social scale, children were set apart from work experience—increasingly they were in school—and, more generally, set apart from the adult world. All kinds of interest, of amusement, of concern now enveloped children. Less and less did they appear as adults in miniature (and in the making); more and more did they seem to constitute a group, a kind of *being,* unto themselves.

This array of new circumstances created a certain awkwardness of transition: how to move from the distinctive experience of childhood to fully adult status? Right there, in the space between childhood and adulthood, lay the years that premoderns had rather vaguely designated as "youth." Only now it was not so vague; in fact, youth became (in the nineteenth century) a sharp focus of attention and anxiety in its own right. One can see this expressed in the proliferation of a new print genre, loosely termed "advice to youth." (There occurred at roughly the same time a parallel proliferation of books on parenting, to reflect the new sense of singularity surrounding childhood.) What, then, did "youth" need to be "advised" about? Broadly speaking, it all concerned *choices:* how to make sound, shrewd, and lastingly effective choices from amidst the multiple options that modern life increasingly, and bewilderingly, presented to the young.[24] The options were about work ("careers" in the narrow sense); they were about friends and colleagues (again and again, the advice to youth sounded dire warnings against falling in with "evil companions"); they were about courtship and marriage; they were about what we would call lifestyle; they were about almost anything and everything.

Make the right choices, and good things will come to you. Make bad choices, or perhaps just drift along, and your outlook is definitely bleak.

This factor of options and choices was fundamental to much in the culture—especially the family culture—of the nineteenth century. And increasingly it touched even very young lives. Consider an image, a watercolor painting from about 1820, entitled "The Age of Choice."[25] The painting shows a boy of about four years old strategically seated before a table on which is arranged a purse, a silver knife, a pair of dice, and a piece of fruit. Apparently, the little fellow was supposed to select one or another of these objects in order to indicate his future course; the purse would point to commerce (business), the silver knife to the life of a gentleman, the fruit to farming, the dice to gambling. Four years old, mind you! Clearly, this is not the same as a twenty-year-old deciding on a career or a college education or some such. It's more like fortune-telling perhaps; but it does reflect a similar preoccupation with the variety of possible futures confronting the young (of whatever age). And nothing comparable was pressed on young people in the earlier—the clearly premodern—period.

What was it about choice that had become so intensely problematic? To speak, again, in a very generalized way: there was, first, the real and remarkable broadening of life possibilities in nineteenth-century America; and second (nicely dovetailing with the first), the evident fact that one's elders, most importantly one's parents, no longer provided effective models on which to envision the future. This last element was directly reflected in the autobiographies. Typically a writer described his father as being unhelpful, and sometimes as an outright impediment, in the development of a life plan.[26] Then, too, there was that much-emphasized moment of leaving home, which seemed in every sense a departure—and thus a further comment on the unhelpfulness of parental models.

These bits and pieces of family history return us to the matter of circles and lines. The old way, the cyclical way, as it specifically embraced the shape of life, involved a nice, even, curving flow in which the parts shaded gently from one to the next. In fact, the parts were themselves only loosely distinguished. The newer configuration—and we needn't call it a cycle anymore—involved parts that were chopped off at either end, and that presented varying forms of contrast with one another. It included, moreover, the grown-up parts, of which we made a good deal before. The gist is that a gathering trend began to express those parts— in effect, to *congeal* those parts—as "middle age," as just another life stage, and not the culminating fulfillment of personhood.[27] Admittedly, the process was very gradual, and almost invisible; it wouldn't stand fully clear until sometime in the twentieth century.

Considered all together, the changes that most vividly involved the first few decades of life opened a door to a more linear configuration. Individuals could put the parts together in different ways; and the anxiety around youth in particular reflected a new openness in the variety of lines leading on toward the future. (Again, please remember: not necessarily straight lines. And not necessarily upward lines, either; things could also go down, way down. The boy be-

side the table, at his "age of choice," might grab the dice—
and thus become destined to the dreaded, and dreadful, life
of a gambler.)

We must acknowledge, finally, some important lines of
difference in relation to all this—and even of outright exclu-
sion. One involved gender, for it does seem that "the rise of
the linear" was primarily a *male* phenomenon. Not entirely;
some of those autobiographies, described above, are by
women. Moreover, their authors appear to share in, and
support, the linear goals of the men to whom they are connected. Yet, on second thought, such support served mostly
to maintain elements of the traditional, circular world—
which would then allow the menfolk to head out more
confidently on a linear course. Surely, it's no coincidence
that the heavily idealized Home of that time-period, the
Home that served as "a haven in a heartless world," was typically figured in circular ways: for example, the "circle of
the hearth," indeed the "family circle" itself. And invariably,
by the same reckoning, Home was women's essential do-
main.[28]

So, too, did race and class cut across the predominant
grain. For the vast majority of African-Americans who were
(until the Civil War) enslaved, there could be no meaningful prospect of molding a long-term, personally distinctive, biographical profile. The entire dimension of widening
choice was closed to them; slaves were formally consigned to
birth, life, and death in the same basic situation—often
enough, literally in the same place. Neither cyclical nor linear figures could reasonably describe such confined, and
confining, experience.

Among the freeborn, mostly white majority, it was especially those in the "middling ranks" who exemplified the

new life patterns. Extreme poverty was usually a barrier to the forms of self-consciousness and self-assertion that fostered a linear outlook, and was no less inhibiting of personal choice. Ironically, individuals at the opposite end of the social spectrum might also stand apart here. Especially in the later nineteenth century would certain "old stock Americans," in their "bastions of privilege," exalt inherited tradition over mobility and change: not for them the linear mode.

But they were standing against an irresistible tide. The circles-to-lines transformation flowed out from its eighteenth-century sources, strengthened more and more by all the social currents we now describe as "modernization." Its initially distinctive American stamp, produced by indigenous (and unprecedented) Revolution, gradually blurred as history at large began to follow a similar track. The forces promoting linearity were as broad as urbanization and capitalism (notwithstanding the matter of business "cycles") and as specific as the invention of the electric light bulb (the single most important precondition of our 24/7 lifestyle). The African student who, in 1961, yearned to associate himself with American "newness" in effect proclaimed the worldwide triumph of linear values.

To this point, we've attempted to build a *social* historian's case for "the rise of the linear": first, by exploring the personal dimension through diaries, autobiographies, and the like, then by forging connections to family history and the life cycle. (To be sure, we're no longer calling it the life cycle; how about "life course" instead? That does seem to capture something of the change.)

Perhaps our chief remaining task is to identify certain

pathways that cross the murky boundary between social history and its closest neighbors, cultural and intellectual history. For such pathways there surely are, leading from all we've previously discussed to fundamental nineteenth-century ideals and values, and even to aspects of personal style. Some of this is so basic and obvious that it may seem trite when flagged in an explicit way. However, there can be no doubt of its importance to all sorts of nineteenth-century folk—of the hope it inspired, the energy it released, the excitement it brought to everyday life. How about "the cult of the self-made man"? Does that sound trite? Perhaps so; however, both concept and phrasing—"self-made man"—were everywhere.[29] Supposedly invented by Henry Clay in 1832 for a speech on the Senate floor, it caught on instantly and became a kind of talisman for orators and writers all over the country. It was there in the titles of best-selling books right through to the end of the century. Here are a few examples, just so we hear the music: John Frost, *Self-Made Men of America* (1848); Charles Seymour, *Self-Made Men* (1858); James McCabe, *Great Fortunes and How They Were Made: or The Struggles and Triumphs of Our Self-Made Men* (1871); and Grover Cleveland (right after completing his second term as president), *The Self-Made Man in American Life* (1897). It was an especially powerful theme on the lecture circuit, too; Frederick Douglass's most successful speech, one that he apparently gave over and over, was entitled simply "Self-Made Men."

With Douglass we can briefly note a particular connection to the history of slavery—and, more especially, of antislavery. Some of the moral energy that eventually tipped the balance against slavery was owing to the way slaves missed the chance for "self-making" (which white Americans regarded as an absolute birthright). The same factor also underlay the huge impact of Douglass's famous autobiographical narrative: where else could one find such a compelling example of this whole ideal than in the story of a man who began life as a slave and proceeded to *make himself* free?[30]

The ideal—the cult—of self-making was, of course, all bound up with concurrent notions of "success," including the acquisition of wealth. But historians of American popular culture have repeatedly sought to remind us that for most nineteenth-century folk this was about more than money, quite a lot more. In certain, more genteel versions it was described as "self-culture," a term made famous by William Ellery Channing and then enthusiastically taken up by Walt Whitman among others.[31] From self-culture it is but a short step to "self-improvement," yet another term with much period currency. Improvement was, for sure, in the air—the nineteenth-century American air. We can give brief acknowledgment, at this point, to reform movements, utopian communities, and the whole spirit of (what they called) perfectionism. And, again: not just improving society, also improving *self*—another acknowledgment, then, of lyceums, the Chatauqua movement, and innumerable, singular, ad hoc efforts of the same sort. Dip into the nineteenth-century records of almost any local community and you find folks endlessly going to lectures, study groups, "recitations." And the subject, the goal, was usually "improvement," in one aspect or another.[32] In fact, we should note some historical change in the meaning of the word itself. Not as dramatic a change as with certain other words considered here ("revolution" and "career"); still, it was enough to be significant. "Improvement," in its seventeenth- and eighteenth-century context, meant "making good use of" one or another resource; you improved your land by growing crops, and harvesting them, and eating them for dinner. But in the nineteenth century "improvement" came to mean what it still means today: simply, making something better—intrinsically better—than before.[33]

It hardly needs saying that all these trends and tendencies were linear to their core. "Self-making" meant moving away from one's point of origin, the farther the better. And that thought can be linked to something mentioned previously as a recurrent element in nineteenth-century autobiographies: the difficulty writers recalled in their relation to their own fathers. To be self-made meant, in the family context, to leave behind, to out-do, and (implicitly, at least) to reject one's father. Therefore, from a Freudian viewpoint, self-making was an oedipal scenario. Father no longer served as a guide or a model—that would be the "cyclical" way. Instead, he became a rival.[34]

Indeed, these connectives—between "the rise of the linear" and the structure and texture of nineteenth-century culture—go on and on. Some quite literally involve space, the organization and configuration of life on the ground. Domestic architecture, for example, moved over time from the organic, center-chimney framed houses of the colonial period (without hallways, and with interior movement following circular patterns) to the much more linear Georgian style of the early national period. Something similar was true of town planning: there the sequence began with the classic premodern pattern of highways and byways encircling a central "green" (or "commons") and ended in the cross-hatched grids of nineteenth-century cities.

My first college-level history course was officially titled "The History of the Westward Movement"; in effect, the very shape of the continent seemed to promote linearity. And consider, too, in roughly the same connection, the whole nineteenth-century "transportation revolution": turnpikes, canals, railroads. Maybe railroads, most of all— what more vivid figure than a line of track extending to the horizon? And let's add to this picture a steam-driven locomotive, to epitomize the energy involved. (The English traveler Frederick Marryat noted in about 1840 that "Americans are a restless, locomotive people," thus gathering engines and humans into the same image.)[35] How about the development of the postal service and the telegraph (with its system of transmission lines)? And newspapers that concentrated on printing actual news, instead of recycling material from one another or from books and related sources that were many generations old (as was typically true with the newspapers of a century before).

Intellectual history, too: for example, the two master idea-systems of the nineteenth century, Marxism and Darwin's evolution. This is a good moment, perhaps, to remind ourselves that the circles-to-lines theme had many transnational connections. Some parts, like self-making, carried a distinctively American flavor; other parts, like the spreading influence of Marx and Darwin, would become worldwide. Last but not least—how could we possibly resist?—even sports (or, to put it more formally, the growth of American sports culture). Behold "our national pastime," indisputably the most wonderful game the world has ever seen—also the oldest American game, and the only one with authentically premodern roots, where the action is not measured by any clock and where the aim is to circle the bases and come *home.* Contrast to baseball the more modern game of football, with its precisely calibrated linear time, where each side tries to march down a long field into an *end zone.*

The baseball/football comparison suggests a segue into an absolutely concluding comment. After three long discussions of life's "circles and lines," it may be reasonable to ask about the discussant's own feelings on the subject; anyway, I'm asking myself. And I'm remembering certain parts of my process in preparing these essays, including a lot of reading. Among the various books I came across, perhaps the best was one by Stephen Jay Gould entitled *Time's Arrow, Time's Cycle.*[36] Most of it is about the history of scientific ideas, as we would expect with Gould. But near the end he strikes a different, more philosophical, even personal, note. Here is what he says: "Time's arrow and time's cycle is, if you will, a 'great' dichotomy because each of its poles captures, by its essence, a theme so central to intellectual (and practical) life that . . . people who hope to understand history must wrestle intimately with both—for time's arrow is the intelligibility of distinct and irreversible events, while time's cycle is the intelligibility of timeless order and lawlike structure. We must have both."[37] I couldn't agree more. In fact, in all its details and particular inflections, this seems just about perfect. Two kinds of "intelligibility" with which to "wrestle intimately," and "we must have both."

This book, too, will close on a personal note. Most of my own life, certainly my younger life, was organized in a pretty linear way. But then, starting around fifteen years ago, the pattern began to change. I couldn't have put a word on it back then; but "circles" does, now, seem to get pretty close. Part of the change, for sure, has been age-related—just getting older. Part of it is being partnered for a very long time with someone who is usually ahead of me on The Big Questions. (After a while I do start to catch up.) And other parts seem almost fortuitous: for example, moving to live in the country, which my wife and I did in the mid-1990s after being lifelong city-dwellers. (In fact, it's astonishing what a difference that change of environment makes.) I'd like to be able to put other words out front here—to explain better what the "circles" piece finally means. But these are very deep waters. Something about beauty, I guess. And connectedness. And acceptance—in the fullest possible sense of that word—*acceptance* of the way things are. I don't regret my many years of linear living. But when all is said and done, with circles and lines—we must indeed have *both*.

Notes

Index

Notes

1. The Traditional World and the Logic of Circularity

1. Ralph Waldo Emerson, "Circles," in *Selections from Ralph Waldo Emerson,* Stephen E. Whicher, ed. (Boston, 1960), 168.

2. This document is reprinted in *Remarkable Providences: Readings on Early American Culture,* rev. ed., John Demos, ed. (Boston, 1991), 294–98.

3. The alternation of waking and sleep experience is but one of many biologically based "circadian rhythms" in all our waking lives. On this point, see Edward S. Ayensu and Philip Whitfield, *The Rhythms of Life* (New York, 1982), 11ff.

4. Quoted in John Demos, *Entertaining Satan: Witchcraft and the Culture of Early New England* (New York, 1982), 132–33, 360, 45.

5. For a good summary of the large literature on this subject, see Jo Ellen Barnett, *Time's Pendulum: The Quest to Capture Time, from Sundials to Atomic Clocks* (New York, 1998). See also Michael O'Malley, *Keeping Watch: A History of American Time* (New York, 1990); David S. Landes, *Revolution in Time: Clocks and the*

Making of the Modern World, rev. ed. (Cambridge, MA, 2000); Michael G. Flaherty, *A Watched Pot: How We Experience Time* (New York, 1999); Gerhard Dohrn-Van Rossum, *A History of the Hour: Clocks and Modern Temporal Orders* (Chicago, 1996).

6. Lewis Mumford, *Technics and Civilization* (New York, 1934), 17.

7. John Nathan Hutchins, *Hutchins Improved: Being an Almanack and Ephemeris of the Motions of the Sun and Moon . . . For the Year of Our Lord 1804* (New York, 1804), front cover.

8. Seaborn Cotton, Commonplace Book (ms. original at the New England Historic Genealogical Society, Boston, MA). Selections are reprinted in Demos, ed., *Remarkable Providences,* 439–46.

9. See George Lyman Kittredge, *Witchcraft in Old and New England* (Cambridge, MA, 1929).

10. Robert Blair St. George, "'Set Thine House in Order': The Domestication of the Yeomanry in Seventeenth-Century New England," in *New England Begins: The Seventeenth Century,* Jonathan L. Fairbanks and Robert F. Trent, eds., three vols. (Boston, 1982), 175–76, 325; see also Darrett B. Rutman and Anita H. Rutman, *A Place in Time: Middlesex County, Virginia, 1650–1750* (New York, 1984), 41–43.

11. Sarah F. McMahon, "'All Things in Their Proper Season': Rhythms of Diet in Nineteenth-Century New England," ms. paper for the Agricultural History Society, International Conference, 1988.

12. David Cressy, "The Seasonality of Marriage in Old and New England," *Journal of Interdisciplinary History,* 16 (1988), 1–21; Samuel T. Brainerd, "Understanding the Seasonality of Marriage: A Case-Study of Seventeenth-Century New England," ms. paper, Duquesne History Forum, 1988.

13. James Henretta, *The Evolution of American Society, 1700–*

1815: An Interdisciplinary Analysis (Lexington, MA, 1973), 33; Kenneth A. Lickridge, "The Conception Cycle as a Tool of Historical Analysis," ms. paper, Stony Brook Conference on Social History, 1969.

14. Robert V. Wells, *Revolutions in Americans' Lives: A Demographic Perspective on the History of America* (Westport, CT, 1982), 32–35, and unpublished research by the author.

15. Rev. John Williams, pastor at Deerfield, MA. His correspondence on this point is quoted in John Demos, *The Unredeemed Captive: A Family Story from Early America* (New York, 1994), 171.

16. John Demos, "Towards a History of Mid-Life: Preliminary Notes and Reflections," in Demos, *Past, Present, and Personal: The Family and the Life Course in American History* (New York, 1986), 114–38.

17. Anne Bradstreet, "The Four Ages of Man," in *The Works of Anne Bradstreet,* Jeannine Hensley, ed. (Cambridge, MA, 1967), 51–63.

18. This argument is more fully presented in Demos, "Toward a History of Mid-Life," 128–30.

19. See Peter Gay, *A Loss of Mastery: Puritan Historians in Colonial America* (Berkeley, CA, 1966); Ernest Lee Tuveson, *Redeemer Nation: The Idea of America's Millennial Role* (Chicago, 1968).

2. The Transitional World and the Power of Novelty

1. The literature on this subject is vast. For starters, see Howard Mumford Jones, *O Strange New World: American Culture, the Formative Years* (New York, 1964); Edmundo O'Gorman, *The Invention of America: An Inquiry into the Historical Nature of the New World* (Westport, CT, 1961); Tzvetan Todorov, *The Conquest of America: The Question of the Other* (New York, 1984).

2. Richard Frethorne, Letter to His Parents, 3 April 1623, reprinted in *Remarkable Providences,* Demos, ed., 46–51.

3. William Bradford, *Of Plymouth Plantation,* Samuel Eliot Morison, ed. (New York, 1952), 23.

4. *The Diary of Cotton Mather,* Worthington Chauncey Ford, ed., two vols. (Boston, n.d.), I, 329.

5. Edward Johnson, *Johnson's Wonder-Working Providence, 1628–1651 (1654)* repr., J. Franklin Jameson, ed. (New York, 1910), 210.

6. The classic work on "declension" is Perry Miller, *The New England Mind: The Seventeenth Century* (New York, 1939), and *The New England Mind: From Colony to Province* (Cambridge, MA, 1953).

7. Cotton Mather, *Magnalia Christi Americana* (London, 1702), repr. Thomas Robbins, ed., two vols. (Boston, 1853–55), I, 1.

8. Letter from Samuel Smith to his son, 1 January 1699, reprinted in *Remarkable Providences,* Demos, ed., 54–56.

9. *The Diary of Samuel Sewall,* M. Halsey Thomas, ed., two vols. (New York, 1973), II, 1046. The Anne Pollard portrait is discussed (with a photographic image) in *New England Begins: The Seventeenth Century,* Jonathan L. Fairbanks and Robert F. Trent, eds., three vols. (Boston, MA, 1982), III, 475.

10. Quoted in Stephen Carl Arch, *After Franklin: The Emergence of Autobiography in Post-Revolutionary America, 1780–1830* (Hanover, NH, 2001), 102–3.

11. See, for example, Bernard Bailyn, *Ideological Origins of the American Revolution* (Cambridge, MA, 1967), and Gordon S. Wood, *The Creation of the American Republic, 1776–1787* (Chapel Hill, NC, 1969).

12. Jay Fliegelman, *Prodigals and Pilgrims: The American Revolution against Patriarchal Authority, 1750–1800* (Cambridge, England, 1982); Peter Shaw, *American Patriots and the Rituals of Revo-*

lution (Cambridge, MA, 1981). See also Gordon S. Wood, *The Radicalism of the American Revolution* (New York, 1992); and Edwin G. Burrows and Michael Wallace, "The American Revolution: The Ideology and Psychology of National Liberation," in *Perspectives in American History,* VI (1972), 223, 239, and *passim.*

13. Shaw, *American Patriots and the Rituals of Revolution,* 187.

14. Thomas Paine, *Common Sense;* J. Hector St. John de Crevecoeur, *Letters from an American Farmer,* Susan Manning, ed. (New York, 1997), 43–44.

15. On Webster, and other advocates for an "Americanized" language, see Jill Lepore, *A Is for American: Letters and Other Characters in the Newly United States* (New York, 2002).

16. Estwick Evans, *Evans' Pedestrious Tour of Four Thousand Miles* (Concord, NH, 1919), 12.

17. Jon Butler, *Becoming America: The Revolution before 1776* (Cambridge, MA, 2000).

18. My summary of this semantical history is based on Hannah Arendt, *On Revolution* (New York, 1962), 34–40; Christopher Hill, "The Word 'Revolution,'" in Hill, *A Nation of Change of Novelty* (London, 1990), ch. 5; Reinhart Koselleck, *Futures Past: On the Semantics of Historical Time,* trans. Keith Tribe (Cambridge, MA, 1988), 41–45; Raymond Williams, *Keywords: A Vocabulary of Culture and Society,* rev. ed. (New York, 1983), 270–74.

19. Arendt, *On Revolution,* 38.

20. Louis Hartz, *The Liberal Tradition in America* (New York, 1955); Joyce Appleby, *Liberalism and Republicanism in the Historical Imagination* (Cambridge, MA, 1992).

21. Charles Royster, *A Revolutionary People at War: The Continental Army and the American Character, 1775–1783* (Chapel Hill, NC, 1979), 8. See also Appleby, *Liberalism and Republicanism in the Historical Imagination,* 8–9, 29ff.

22. Ibid., 32.

23. Winthrop D. Jordan, "Familial Politics: Thomas Paine and the Killing of the King, 1776," *Journal of American History,* 60 (1973), 290–312.

24. Burrows and Wallace, "The American Revolution: The Ideology and Psychology of National Liberation."

25. *Philip Vickers Fithian: Journal, 1775–1776,* Robert G. Albion and Leonidas Dodson, eds. (Princeton, NJ, 1934), 64 (entry of 20 July 1775).

26. See Donald Weber, *Rhetoric and History in Revolutionary New England* (New York, 1988), 152, 154, and *passim.*

27. Royster, *A Revolutionary People at War,* 129.

28. Ibid., 7–8, 16, 33, 97, 160, and *passim.*

29. Ibid., 367–68.

30. Quoted in Arch, *After Franklin,* 37.

31. See, for example, Arch, *After Franklin;* Weber, *Rhetoric and History in Revolutionary New England;* G. Thomas Couser, *Altered Egos: Authority in American Autobiography* (New York, 1989); *First-Person Singular: Studies in American Autobiography,* A. Robert Lee, ed. (New York, 1988); Thomas L. Gustafson, *Representative Words: Politics, Literature, and the American Language* (New York, 1992); Cathy N. Davidson, *Revolution and the Word: The Rise of the Novel in America* (New York, 1986); Larzer Ziff, *Writing in the New Nation: Prose, Print, and Politics in the Early United States* (New Haven, CT, 1991).

32. On these points I am indebted to Arch, *After Franklin* (see esp. 34ff., 40, 124–25), Weber, *Rhetoric and History in Revolutionary New England* (esp. 6, 94–95, 152), and Ziff, *Writing in the New Nation* (esp. 55ff.).

33. Royster, *A Revolutionary People at War,* 245–46.

34. Alfred F. Young, *The Shoemaker and the Tea Party: Memory and the American Revolution* (Boston, MA, 1999).

3. The Modern World and the Rise of the Linear

1. Kathleen Donegan, Ph.D. dissertation in progress (American Studies Department, Yale University); I am grateful for the opportunity to consult this work.

2. Oscar Handlin, *The Uprooted* (Boston, 1951). See also Handlin, "The Significance of the Seventeenth Century," in *Seventeenth-Century America: Essays in Colonial History,* James Morton Smith, ed. (Chapel Hill, NC, 1959), 3–12.

3. The best available study of this material is David S. Shields, "A History of Personal Diary-Writing in New England, 1620–1745" (Ph.D. dissertation, University of Chicago, 1982).

4. I am grateful to Molly McCarthy (Brandeis University) for allowing me to consult her work in progress on early American almanacs.

5. See *Remarkable Providences: Readings on Early American History,* John Demos, ed., rev. ed. (Boston, 1991), 59–69.

6. Anne Bradstreet, "To My Dear Children," in *The Works of Anne Bradstreet,* Jeannine Hensley, ed. (Cambridge, MA, 1967), 240; Thomas Shepard, autobiography, in *God's Plot: The Paradoxes of Puritan Piety,* Michael McGiffert, ed. (Amherst, MA, 1972), 33.

7. I am here indebted (again) to Joyce Appleby's recent work. Her excellent book *Inheriting the Revolution: The First Generation of Americans* (Cambridge, MA, 2000) is based, in large part, on a reading of some 400 autobiographies written in the post-Revolutionary period. In addition, Appleby has edited and published a very useful collection of excerpts from these documents: *Recollections of the Early Republic: Selected Autobiographies* (Boston, 1997).

8. The quantitative upsurge can itself be seen as a result of political and social change growing out of the Revolution. Literature scholars have posited "a special compatibility between American

culture and autobiographical discourse." (G. Thomas Course, *Altered Egos: Authority in American Autobiography* [New York, 1992], 13.) Their fundamental point is that "for many Americans the promise of the new republic is [and was] that anyone can write the definitive account of his or her own life." (Ibid., 12.) And again: "Autobiography . . . does seem to be a form peculiarly suited to the traditional American self-image: individualistic and optimistic." (Thomas Doherty, "American Autobiography and Ideology," quoted in ibid., 13.)

9. On the history of the self, see, for example, Gerald N. Izenberg, *Impossible Individuality: Romanticism, Revolution, and the Origins of Modern Selfhood* (Princeton, NJ, 1992), and Charles Taylor, *Sources of the Self: The Making of Modern Identity* (Cambridge, MA, 1989).

10. See *Recollections of the Early Republic,* Appleby, ed., 4–5.

11. Ibid., 136, 162, 43.

12. Ibid., 56.

13. Ibid., 167, 164, 167.

14. Ibid., 40.

15. Sarah Buell Hale, quoted in Appleby, *Inheriting the Revolution,* 167.

16. *Recollections of the Early Republic,* Appleby, ed., 14.

17. What I know about the history of ambition comes largely from the work of Casey King; I am grateful for the chance to consult his dissertation in progress (American Studies Department, Yale University).

18. *Recollections of the Early Republic,* Appleby, ed., 165, 166, 182.

19. *Exploring Affect: The Selection Writings of Silvan S. Tomkins,* E. Virginia Demos, ed. (New York, 1995), 57ff.

20. Stephen Carl Arch, *After Franklin: The Emergence of Autobiography in Post-Revolutionary America, 1780–1830* (Hanover, NH, 2001).

21. Ibid. Franklin's autobiography can be found in *The Writings of Benjamin Franklin,* A. Leo LeMay, ed. (New York, 1987), 1303–1469.

22. On the history of the word "career," see Raymond Williams, *Keywords: A Vocabulary of Culture and Society,* rev. ed. (New York, 1983), 52–54. On the changing reality of American careers, see Appleby, *Inheriting the Revolution,* ch. 4, and Christopher Clark, *The Roots of Rural Capitalism: Western Massachusetts, 1780–1860* (Ithaca, NY, 1990), 113–16, 160–63, and *passim.*

23. On childhood in nineteenth-century America, see Bernard Wishy, *The Child and the Republic: The Dawn of Modern American Child Nurture* (Philadelphia, 1972).

24. On expanding choices in nineteenth-century America, see Daniel Walker Howe, *Making the American Self: Jonathan Edwards to Abraham Lincoln* (Cambridge, MA, 1997), 110–11 and *passim.* On the literature of "advice to youth," see Joseph Kett, *Rites of Passage: Adolescence in America, 1790 to the Present* (New York, 1977).

25. For an image of this painting, see Carl W. Dreppard, *American Pioneer Arts and Artists* (Springfield, MA, 1942), 92.

26. Appleby, *Inheriting the Revolution,* 170–74.

27. John Demos, "Towards a History of Mid-Life: Preliminary Notes and Reflections," in Demos, *Past, Present, and Personal: The Family and the Life Course in American History* (New York, 1986), ch. 6.

28. On gender differences in relation to the "linear" aspects of liberalism, see Appleby, *Liberalism and Republicanism in the Historical Imagination,* 29–30. On the idealization of Home, see Christopher Lasch, *Haven in a Heartless World* (New York, 1977).

29. John G. Cawelti, *Apostles of the Self-Made Man* (Chicago, 1965), and Howe, *Making the American Self.*

30. On Douglass and "self-making," see ibid., 149–56.

31. Ibid., 130–35.

32. Ibid., 114–28, 190–91.

33. On the changed meanings of "improvement," see ibid., 122–23, and Williams, *Keywords,* 160–61.

34. See John Demos, "Oedipus and America: Historical Perspectives on the Reception of Psychoanalysis in the United States," in *The Annual of Psychoanalysis,* 6 (1978), 23–39.

35. Quoted in Appleby, *Inheriting the Revolution,* 7.

36. Stephen Jay Gould, *Time's Arrow, Time's Cycle: Myth and Metaphor in the Discovery of Geological Time* (Cambridge, MA, 1987).

37. Ibid., 15–16.

Index

Adams, John, 39
almanacs, 8–9, 62
"ambition," ideas about, 69
annual cycle, 10ff.
Appleby, Joyce, 48, 50
Arch, Stephen Carl, 54, 70
autobiographies, 62ff.

Bailyn, Bernard, 48
Ball, John, 65
Bolingbroke, Lord, 22
"Book of Knowledge," 9–10
Bradford, William, 30, 58
Bradstreet, Anne, 18–19, 64

"career," meanings of, 71
Channing, William Ellery, 79
childhood, 18, 72–74
Clay, Henry, 78
clocks, 8
Columbus, Christopher, 26
conception cycle, 12
Copernicus, 46
Crevecoeur, Hector St John, 40

Dane, John, 62–3, 66
diaries, 60ff.
diet, 11
diurnal cycle, 3–8
Donegan, Kathleen, 58
Douglass, Frederick, 78–9
Drake, Daniel, 66–7
dreams, 6

economy, conceptions of, 22
Edwards, Jonathan, 23
Emerson, Ralph Waldo, 1
Evans, Estwick, 41

Faunce, Thomas, 35
Franklin, Benjamin, 45, 70

Gould, Stephen Jay, 82
governance, conceptions of,
   22

Handlin, Oscar, 59
Harding, Chester, 66
Hartz, Louis, 48

Index

Hewes, George Robert Twelves, 55–6
history, conceptions of, 22, 49

"improvement," meanings of, 79
infancy, 18

Jefferson, Thomas, 38
Jerome, Chauncey, 66
Jones, Howard Mumford, 28

Lee, Henry, 38
liberalism, 49
life cycle, 15ff., 72ff.
lunar cycle, 8–9

marriage, seasonality of, 11–12
Marryat, Frederick, 81
Massachusetts, General Court, 2
Mather, Cotton, 10, 31, 33–4
middle age, 18, 75
millennialism, 23–4
"moonlighting," 9
mortality, seasonality of, 14–15
Mumford, Lewis, 7

novelty, and American history, 25–6, 30ff., 39ff., 58–9

Paine, Thomas, 39, 47
place-names, in colonial America, 31–2
Pocock, John, 48
Pollard, Anne, 35

"providences," 21, 60
Puritanism, 23, 30–1, 60–1

republicanism, 48
"revolution," meanings of, 45–7
Revolution, American, 37–8, 45ff.
Revolution, French, 47
Royster, Charles, 53, 55

"self-culture," 79
"self-improvement," 79
"self-made man," 78
Sewall, Samuel, 35
Shakespeare, William, 6
Shepard, Thomas, 64
slavery, 77–9
sports, 81–2
Stiles, Ezra, 53
sundials, 8

time, measurement of, 2–3, 7

Webster, Noah, 40
Whitman, Walt, 79
Winthrop, John, 30
witchcraft, 4
women, and childbearing, 9; and court cases, 19; and the life cycle, 76; and the menses, 9, 19–20
Wood, Gordon, 48
work, rhythms of, 2, 10–11

Young, Alfred F., 55
"youth," 18, 73